Leading the Way to Excellence in AT Services

A GUIDE FOR SCHOOL ADMINISTRATORS

GAYL BOWSER *and* **PENNY R. REED**

Library of Congress Control Number 2018951310

Paperback ISBN 978-1-930583-10-8
Ebook ISBN 978-1-930583-11-5

Published by
CAST Professional Publishing
an imprint of CAST, Inc.
Wakefield, MA 01880
www.cast.org

Cover and interior design by Happenstance Type-O-Rama.

Printed in the United States of America.

Contents

About the Authors

GAYL BOWSER, MSEd, is an independent education consultant and mentor. Her work focuses on the creation of service systems that encourage the integration of technology into educational programs for students with disabilities. Formerly the coordinator of the Oregon Technology Access Program (OTAP) and Oregon's state specialist in assistive technology (AT), Gayl is credentialed in Oregon as an administrator-school superintendent. She currently provides AT consultation, professional development, and technical assistance throughout the United States and internationally.

PENNY R. REED, PhD, has a BS in elementary education, and master and doctoral degrees in special education. She has been a teacher, consultant, and administrator in the field of special education and AT. Penny regularly provides consultation and training on a variety of topics related to AT assessment and service delivery with a special focus on helping school districts improve their delivery of assistive technology services.

Gayl Bowser and Penny Reed are coauthors of numerous publications about AT services, including the books *Education Tech Points: A Framework for Assistive Technology*, *Assistive Technology Pointers for Parents*, and *Quality Indicators for Assistive Technology: A Comprehensive Guide to Assistive Technology Services*, and (with the QIAT Leadership Team) *Quality Indicators for Assistive Technology: A Comprehensive Guide to Assistive Technology Services.*

Introduction

Leading the Way to Excellence in AT Services: A Guide for School Administrators is a "how-to" guide for educators who want to develop or improve assistive technology (AT) services for their schools, districts, programs, or agencies. It includes several self-assessment tools that can help leaders focus efforts on actions that have been proven successful and that fit into the routine tasks that administrators and AT leaders commonly do.

This book is intended for two audiences: educational administrators and AT providers. Educational administrators include principals, assistant principals, special education directors, special education supervisors, and anyone else filling a position of leadership in the schools. AT providers include individuals with *assistive technology* in their job title or job description as well as those who love technology and find themselves helping others figure out how to use it. These two audiences work together in order to develop truly effective and efficient AT services for students with disabilities.

Administrators have specific responsibilities that contribute to the successful provision and implementation of AT for individual students. Successful programs begin with a vision of what quality services should look like. Effective school administrators develop a vision jointly with educators, parents, students, and other community stakeholders. They then set a course of action that helps the agency move toward that vision.

Historically in many educational agencies, AT has not been made part of that vision. The time has come for change so that part of the vision for any educational program is the vision of how AT devices and services can be offered in an effective, legal, ethical, and cost-efficient manner for all students with disabilities to increase their success.

School administrators are the leaders for the program they serve, whether it is a specific program, a building, or an entire agency. In addition to their overall leadership responsibilities, school administrators engage in three types of activities: (a) they manage the programs for which they have responsibility; (b) they supervise the staff employed in these programs; and (c) they lead program development and improvement efforts.

Providing effective AT services requires a school administrator to address assistive technology from each of these administrative perspectives. As managers, school administrators sign purchase orders for new equipment and ensure consistent and equitable services. As supervisors, school administrators ensure that the agency has qualified staff members who are knowledgeable about AT and the technology needs of students with disabilities. As leaders in program development, school administrators include AT in long-term planning efforts.

In an international synthesis of research about successful school leadership, Leithwood, Harris, & Hopkins (2008) noted that almost all successful leaders draw on the same set of basic leadership practices. They organized these into four categories:

- building vision and setting directions,

- managing the program,

- understanding and developing individuals, and

- redesigning the organization.

This book will look closely at each of these four aspects of successful leadership in order to help administrators identify critical issues and specific actions that will influence the provision of AT devices and services.

After reading this book, we hope that you will be able to

- identify ways that you can directly support educational programs that encourage and sustain students' and educators' use of AT;

- create and share a vision of your agency's approach to providing AT devices and services;

- manage material resources, allocation of personnel, time, and physical resources in a way that helps provide an efficient, ethical, and cost-effective system for AT;

- support educators in learning and applying pedagogical strategies for integrating the use of AT into the educational programs of students with disabilities; and

- regularly assess AT services and identify strategies to improve the current model.

Almost every person who reads this book uses technology for a variety of tasks every day. In many cases, technology changes the quality of work produced and increases productivity. Many school districts provide AT to a large portion of their students with disabilities. But many more struggle to provide AT to even a small number of their students with disabilities. Given the significant impact that the use of technology can have, how can the status quo be changed to make it possible to provide AT to all students with disabilities when it is needed? The purpose of this book is to address issues that hold back the provision of AT and to focus on specific leadership steps that can move districts toward high-quality, effective, and cost-efficient AT services.

CHAPTER 1

Understanding Assistive Technology

Use this chapter to make sure that you are knowledgeable about the definitions, legal mandates, and frequently asked questions about AT devices and services provided in public school settings.

- ✔ Know what AT is and how it can benefit students with disabilities.

- ✔ Know the legal definitions of AT, the requirements to provide AT for students with disabilities, and the implications for my program.

- ✔ Be able to answer questions that staff, families, and others frequently ask about your AT services.

DO YOU KNOW ABOUT...

- ☐ the most powerful intervention to help students with disabilities meet Individualized Education Program (IEP) goals?

- ☐ an intervention that can double the graduation rate of your students with mild disabilities?

- ☐ an intervention that can have a powerful impact on reading comprehension?

- ☐ an intervention that is effective with 89% of students who struggle with learning to speak?

These are all characteristics of AT. You will find out more about each specific aspect as you read this chapter. Although most AT leaders know a great deal about AT devices, they may not be aware of the requirements of the Individuals with Disabilities Education Improvement Act (IDEA) or the research on the effectiveness of AT.

In the preamble to the IDEA, Congress stated that

Almost 30 years of research and experience has demonstrated that the education of children with disabilities can be made more effective by... (H) supporting the development and use of technology, including assistive technology devices and assistive technology services, to maximize accessibility for children with disabilities.

(p. 118)

Since 2004, when IDEA was first published, awareness of the significant role that technology plays in the education of all children has increased dramatically. The recent National Education Technology Plan (NETP; Office of Educational Technology, 2017) states that one of the main goals of education is that "All learners will have engaging and empowering learning experiences in both formal and informal settings that prepare them to be active, creative, knowledgeable, and ethical participants in our globally connected society."

The NETP goes on to point out the numerous ways that technology makes this possible, including the importance of AT in making learning accessible to all students. In the NETP recommendations, AT is identified as part of the vision for effective technology use. The first NETP recommendation is

States, districts, and postsecondary institutions should develop and implement learning resources that embody the flexibility and power of technology to create equitable and accessible learning ecosystems that make learning possible everywhere and all the time for all students.

(Office of Educational Technology, 2017, p. 25)

That powerful recommendation is backed up by research. The National Longitudinal Transition Study-2 (Bouck, 2016) looked at postsecondary outcomes for students nationally and found that students with high incidence disabilities who received AT performed significantly better than those who did not receive AT (Table 1.1).

TABLE 1.1.

Postsecondary outcomes for students with high-incidence disabilities

OUTCOME	STUDENTS WHO RECEIVED AT	STUDENTS WITHOUT AT
Graduation	99.8%	79.6%
Postsecondary enrollment	80.9%	40.1%
Paying job	80%	50.8%

Looking at AT's impact another way, Watson, Ito, Smith, and Anderson (2010) found that beginning to use AT resulted in improvement in meeting IEP goals and objectives by students who were having difficulty achieving progress with standard classroom interventions. The study also suggested that the contribution of AT as an intervention strategy is greater than any of the other possible intervention strategies they identified.

Mandates to Provide AT

More than one federal law addresses the requirement that school districts provide assistive technology to students who need it to benefit from and have equal access to their educational programs. Most students with disabilities receive their AT under the mandates in IDEA. However, other students may receive similar AT devices and services under the requirements of Section 504 of the Rehabilitation Act (Section 504) or the Americans with Disabilities Act (ADA).

School districts have been required since 1990 to provide both AT devices and services. IDEA states

Each public agency shall ensure that assistive technology devices or assistive technology services, or both, as those terms are defined in §300.5–300.6, are made available to a student with a disability if required as a part of the student's

Special education under §300.26;

Related services under §300.24; or

Supplementary aids and services under §300.28 and 300.550(b)(2).

(b) On a case-by-case basis, the use of school-purchased assistive technology devices in a student's home or in other settings is required if the student's IEP team determines that the student needs access to those devices in order to receive FAPE.

(34 CFR §300.308 [Authority: 20 U. S. C. § 1412(a)(12)(B)(i)])

This provision requires that the devices and services be available to every student with a disability if that student needs AT in order to receive a free appropriate public education (FAPE). Education agencies are required to provide AT to students with disabilities to ensure that they have access to their educational programs. This access can mean access to special instruction, access to the general curriculum, or access to extracurricular activities.

Part (b) of section 300.308 addresses the use of school-purchased AT at home. When students with disabilities have educational goals that require them to use specific skills at home, the IEP team may decide that the AT also is needed at home—for example, if the student has homework and the AT is needed in order to do the homework. The use of an augmentative communication device may also require home use. One decision that school administrators should participate in making is what would happen if the device that a student takes home is damaged due to neglect or abuse on the part of the family. This is the kind of question that the IEP team cannot answer without direction from an administrator or written procedural guidelines from the education agency.

Guidance about AT provided in Attachment 1 of IDEA states that assistive technology must address

- personal needs for AT devices,
- access to technology commonly used by other students, and
- appropriate involvement in and progress in the general curriculum.

When AT is needed, it becomes part of FAPE for the student. The AT devices that are necessary to ensure FAPE must be provided at no cost to the parents, and the parents cannot be charged for normal use and wear and tear. Conversely, IDEA also states that the provision of AT devices and services is limited to those situations in which they are required in order for a student with disabilities to receive FAPE (34 CFR, Attachment 1). Since 1975, FAPE has been the standard to which school districts are held. Recently the bar has been raised by the Supreme Court. In *Endrew F. vs. Douglas County School District*, the Supreme Court ruled that schools must offer "an IEP reasonably calculated to enable a child to make progress appropriate in light of the child's circumstances" and further that the program should be "appropriately ambitious" and that "every child should have the chance to meet challenging objectives" (Howe, 2017). In many cases, the provision of AT devices and services can be the approach that allows the student to meet more challenging objectives and experience an appropriately ambitious program.

Not all students with disabilities need specially designed instruction. Students with disabilities who do not require specially designed instruction are not eligible for special education services under IDEA and will not have IEPs. These students may still need AT in order to access or participate in their education and may receive it under the provisions of Section 504 of the Rehabilitation Act of 1973 or the Americans with Disabilities Act of 1990 (Title II). Section 504 is a civil rights law that guarantees that no student with a disability will "be excluded from participation in, be denied the benefits of, or be subjected to discrimination under any program or activity receiving Federal financial assistance" (Rehabilitation Act of 1973, Section 504, 1977). Education agencies that receive federal funds must provide accommodations to students with disabilities if needed so that they will receive an education equal to that of their peers. One or more of those accommodations may be AT. There is no required schedule for the consideration or assessment of the needs for AT under Section 504 or Title II. The education agency should have a procedure in place to address the need for AT for students who receive services under Section 504.

The Americans with Disabilities Act (ADA) of 1990 (Title II) is also a civil rights law that prohibits discrimination on the basis of disability. Students with disabilities are covered by Title II and Section 504 regardless of their eligibility for special education and related services under the IDEA. Students who qualify under Section 504 and the ADA are those who: (1) have a physical or mental impairment that substantially limits one or more major life activities, (2) have a record of such an impairment, or (3) are regarded as having such an impairment. State and local education agencies are required by Section 504 and Title II to ensure an equal educational opportunity to students with disabilities, including the timely provision of AT if it is needed.

There are differences between IDEA and the Title II regulations. Title II regulations require that public schools provide appropriate "auxiliary aids and services" when necessary to afford an "equal opportunity" to participate in and benefit from the district's services, programs, and activities. Assistive technology may be part of those "auxiliary aides." Title II specifically requires that a student with disabilities have the opportunity to be as effective at communicating as a student without disabilities (U.S. Department of Justice and U.S. Department of Education, 2014). This is a more stringent requirement than IDEA and may require further action.

AT Devices

What is an AT device? Assistive technology is any tool that helps a student with a disability to complete a task that is difficult or impossible to complete because of the disability. AT can be an adapted pencil, or it can be a tablet computer that allows the student to dictate what she needs to write. It is enlarged text on a colored background or a web-based computer that speaks the text to a student who struggles with decoding. It is a walker that allows a student to move throughout his classroom environment or a power chair that allows him to move throughout his community. The term *assistive technology* refers to a broad range of items. They may be extremely inexpensive or in rare cases, very expensive, but they all function as a tool to help an individual perform a task.

The Individuals with Disabilities Education Act (IDEA) defines an AT device as

any item, piece of equipment, or product system, whether acquired commercially off the shelf, modified, or customized, that is used to increase, maintain, or improve the functional capabilities of a child with a disability. The term does not include a medical device that is surgically implanted, or the replacement of that device.

(34 C.F.R. §300.5 [Authority 20 U.S.C. 1401(1)])

This definition highlights that AT is

- anything (item, piece of equipment, or product system),

- no matter where it comes from (acquired commercially, modified, or customized),

- that helps a student do something he cannot do without it or helps that student do it better than he could do it without it (increase, maintain, or improve a functional capability).

The federal definition of AT begins with the words "any item." Although many devices were originally developed as AT, there are also many common items designed for other uses that can be AT for a specific student. Any item that is required by a student to increase functional capabilities is AT. Functional capabilities are broad areas of skills that are used across environments and for a variety of specific tasks. Here is a list some of the functional capabilities that might be increased, maintained, or improved by the use of AT:

- communicating,
- controlling the environment,
- hearing and listening,
- moving through an environment,
- working with numbers,
- playing,
- reading,
- remembering,
- seeing,
- studying, organizing,
- completing tasks related to employment, and
- writing.

Table 1.2 includes examples of AT for four functional skill areas that are critical to a student's progress in the curriculum. There is AT for every task that students need to do to meet IEP goals and make progress in the curriculum. Looking quickly at the four tasks represented in Table 1.1, it is apparent that all students need to be able to competently complete these tasks, and although communication aids are usually needed only by a student with a severe disability, tools for reading, studying, and composing are relevant for all students, especially those with milder, high-incidence disabilities.

Many people use speech-to-text on their mobile phones because it is fast, but it would not be AT if those people could just as easily key in the information. For a child with a disability who cannot accurately key in the information due to some aspect of her disability, that use of speech-to-text is AT. The same is true for all AT. Many of the items that turn out to be AT for a specific student with a disability are readily available things that many people use.

TABLE 1.2.

AT examples by functional area addressed

READING	STUDYING/INFORMATION MANAGEMENT
Adapted books for access (e.g., page separators)	Paper sticky notes, sticky tabs (e.g., Post-It)
Picture symbol supported text	Highlighters (e.g., markers, highlight tape)
Modified text: size, color, spacing	Low-tech aids to locate (e.g., index tabs, colored folders)
Tracking aids-reading windows/cutouts	Recorded material (e.g., books on tape, taped lectures with number coded index)
Talking electronic dictionaries	Electronic bookmarks and voice notes
Podcasts to summarize or highlight reading	Auto summary in word processing programs
Handheld scanners/readers (e.g., C-Pen Reader, ReadingPen TS)	Electronic organizers
Audio books, MP3 players	Electronic reminders
Digital e-readers (e.g., Kindle, ClassMate Reader)	Handheld scanners/readers (e.g., C-Pen Reader, ReadingPen TS)
Scan and read handheld (e.g., Intel Reader)	Recording/bookmarking pen (e.g., Livescribe smartpen)
Digital books with text highlighted as read	Software for organization of ideas and studying (e.g., Inspiration, Draft:Builder)
Digital books with adapted text (e.g., Start-to-Finish)	Online search tools (e.g., netTrekker, Thinkfinity)
	Online web trackers
	Online sorting file tools (e.g., Sort My List)
	Online animations, interactives, or tutorials

COMPOSITION/SPELLING	COMMUNICATION
Word cards, word book, word wall	Communication board or book with pictures and/or words
Pocket dictionary/thesaurus	Eye-gaze board or frame
Graphic organizer	Simple speech-generating device (SGD; e.g., BIGmack, Go Talk, Step-by-Step)
Talking, electronic dictionary, spell checker	SGD with levels (e.g., Tech Speak)
Word processing with spell/grammar check	SGD with icon sequencing (e.g., Accent, Nova Chat)
Talking word processor	Multilevel SGD including alternative access (e.g., Indi, LightWriter SL40)
Abbreviation/expansion/macros	Tablet computer with communication apps (e.g., Proloquo2Go, TouchChat, Voice4U)
Outlining/mapping software (e.g., Inspiration)	
Word prediction (e.g., Co:Writer, WordQ)	

The impact of AT use will vary but will most likely be one or more of the following:

- increased levels of independence,

- improved quality of life,

- increased productivity,

- enhanced performance on specific tasks,

- reduced fatigue,

- expanded educational or vocational options,

- increased success in general education settings, or

- reduced amount of support services needed.

AT can have that kind of impact only if it is used in the classroom and other educational environments on a regular basis for the completion of important educational tasks.

Common Questions about AT Devices

The wide range of AT devices has led administrators to ask many questions, such as the following.

Is all technology AT?

No. There are drill and practice programs, tutorials, and many other kinds of technology that teachers use in classrooms to enhance their teaching, provide additional practice, or motivate students. Technology used in this way is not AT. One way to understand the difference between instructional technology and assistive technology is to ask the following questions:

What will the tool do for a student?

What would happen to the student if this tool were taken away?

In order to be AT, a device must increase, maintain, or improve a functional capability. If you take AT away from a student with a disability who understands how to use it, the student will find it more difficult or even impossible to perform the task for which it is used. This is because AT acts as a support to help the student overcome the barrier posed by the disability. At the same time, when you take instructional technology away from a student it is likely that the student will not show a decrease in performance. Instructional technology is used to help a student learn new skills, but it is not needed as an ongoing support once those skills are learned.

The needs of each student determine whether an item is considered AT. For example, the entire class may be learning to use word processing as a tool for writing. After becoming proficient, most students in the class will still be able to (and will choose to) use a pencil and paper for some writing tasks. However, some students who have a physical or learning disability in the area of writing may need to use word processing software for all writing tasks. For these students, word processing software increases their functional capability in writing and is AT.

Does the AT requirement of IDEA apply only to certain categories of disability?

No. IDEA makes it clear that every IEP team must consider AT for every student who receives special education services. This includes students with high-incidence disabilities such as learning disabilities and mild cognitive disabilities. Because AT services originated in a medical model, many people still think of it as something separate and unusual. Just as general technology has changed and spread into general use throughout the population, AT has expanded to include thousands of products that can support students with all types of disabilities to be more independent and productive.

Is there research about the effectiveness of assistive technology?

Yes. For example, there is quite a lot of research on the use of text-to-speech for students with learning disabilities. The most recent, comprehensive review by Wood, Moxley, Tighe, and Wagner (2018) found the use of text-to-speech tools has a significant impact on reading comprehension scores for students with learning disabilities, especially those with slow or inaccurate decoding that does not correlate to their cognitive and intellectual potential (i.e., less than 90% accuracy) and lower levels of fluency (i.e., less than 92 words per minute).

Other research shows the benefit of graphic organizers (Hall and Strangman, 2002; Gajria, Jitendra, Sood, & Sacks, 2007), e-books (mostly because the student can change font size) (Siegenthaler, Wurtz, & Groner, 2011), word pre-diction for writing (Silió & Barbetta 2010; Cullen, Richards, & Lawless-Frank, 2008; Tam, Archer, Mays, & Skidmore, 2005), and speech recognition for writing (Quinlan, 2004; MacArthur & Cavalier, 2004; McCollum, Nation, & Gunn, 2014). All can have a significant impact on student performance.

In a review of the research about AT for students with severe disabilities, Browder, Wood, Thompson, and Ribuffo (2014) found that evidence about AT is often woven into more general research about teaching and learning and that within that research there is broad support for the use of AT for this population. For students with severe disabilities, AT can support mobility, positioning, hearing, vision, communication, activities of daily living, and instruction (Spooner, Browder, & Mims, 2011).

If a student uses AT, will she stop learning the basic skill?

No. It is a commonly held misconception that the use of AT will mean that the child will stop learning the basic skill that the AT is being used to support, but there is no research that shows a loss of skills due to the use of AT. Rather, the opposite is true. In a thorough meta-analysis of the literature, Millar, Light, and Schlosser (2006) found that the introduction of AT in the form of augmentative and alternative communication (AAC) to provide voice output did not slow or prevent the development of spoken language. In fact, speech production increased in 89% of the subjects across studies. An earlier study by Schepis, Reid, Behrmann, and Sutton (1998) looked at all types of communicative behavior, not just speech production, and found that the use of a voice output AAC device increased the use of all communication behaviors, including gestures, vocalizations, and word use.

A review of the research about the use of power mobility shows that there are no grounds for the fear that children will regress in motor skills due to its use (Bottos, Bolcati, Sciuto, Ruggeri, & Feliciangeli, 2000; Jones, McEwen, & Hansen, 2003).

Likewise, the introduction of the use of text-to-speech software does not cause a student to stop learning to read. Rather, it increases vocabulary, increases reading speed, and provides repeated exposure to correct pronunciation. Its use leaves more room in active memory for constructing meaning and leaves students less fatigued (Stodden, Roberts, Takahashi, Park, & Stodden, 2012). A recent definitive meta-analysis of the research (Wood et al., 2018) found the use of text-to-speech tools has a significant impact on reading comprehension scores for students with learning disabilities.

Is providing the AT enough?

No. Provision of AT is only a first step. Simply having an AT device does not ensure that a student with a disability will experience increased function. The full range of AT services may be needed to support the student's AT use.

AT Services

The definition of AT devices was included earlier in this chapter. Equally important is the definition of AT services. In IDEA, they are defined as

ASSISTIVE TECHNOLOGY SERVICE–The term "assistive technology service" means any service that directly assists a child with a disability in the selection, acquisition, or use of an assistive technology device.

Such term includes

- *the evaluation of the needs of such child, including a functional evaluation of the child in the child's customary environment;*

- *purchasing, leasing, or otherwise providing for the acquisition of assistive technology devices by such child;*

- *selecting, designing, fitting, customizing, adapting, applying, maintaining, repairing, or replacing of assistive technology devices;*

- *coordinating and using other therapies, interventions, or services with assistive technology devices, such as those associated with existing education and rehabilitation plans and programs;*

- *training or technical assistance for such child, or, where appropriate, the family of such child; and training or technical assistance for professionals (including individuals providing education and rehabilitation services), employers, or other individuals who provide services to, employ, or are otherwise substantially involved in the major life functions of such child.*

(34 CFR § 300.6 [Authority: 20 U.S.C. § 1401(2)])

The first responsibility assigned to school districts is the evaluation of the child's need for AT, including a functional evaluation in that child's customary environments. Use of the term *functional evaluation* is not accidental; it was used to convey the importance of gathering authentic information based on the child's performance while completing meaningful tasks as part of familiar routines and activities in the classroom and other environments where the child is learning. Completing a functional evaluation rather than a standardized test yields more contextually relevant information about a child's strengths and needs (Bagnato, Neisworth, & Pretti-Frontczak, 2010). A functional evaluation yields information that is more relevant to making a decision about the need for AT and is also more culturally sensitive and authentic. Authenticity is critical as the more realistic the task, the more applicable the results will be to everyday routines and activities (Delaney, 1999). These terms were carefully chosen by Congress to impress on school districts the need to carry out AT evaluations, rather than referring the child to an outside agency on a routine basis.

The remaining required assistive technology services listed in IDEA relate to obtaining the needed AT, training the child and all of the individuals who will support the child's use of AT, and generally ensuring that AT is available and used. The list of AT services is brief, but the words include a number of important ideas and concepts. IDEA also indicates that any other service that is needed to help a child select, acquire, or use AT must be provided by the education agency.

The Importance of Teams in AT Services

Several types of teams play a critical role in the delivery of AT services no matter what type of AT device is being used, the age or disability of the student, or the size or wealth of the education agency. These include the following:

- The IEP team—Required by law, all decisions about a student's individual educational program are made by a team, including decisions about the student's need for AT.

- The student services team—The team of people who provide all of the educational and related services to a student. It includes the members of the IEP team plus any other individuals who provide services to the student. For example, additional members might include other teachers, related services providers, and instructional assistants.

- The Assistive Technology team—A team of individuals with some knowledge about AT who may work directly with students to conduct AT evaluations and training or may support others throughout the agency to perform those tasks, providing training and technical assistance to develop the capacity of all members of student services teams throughout the agency.

There are several reasons why AT services are generally provided by a team:

- Assistive technology is often used across several environments, thus requiring individuals in those environments to be involved in its use.

- Assistive technology crosses several disciplines. There is no single expert who knows everything that is needed to effectively implement AT.

- Input from multiple sources during planning and problem solving can avoid problems and be cost effective.

- Teams help distribute the workload in a way that is both effective and efficient.

Since AT was first mandated in IDEA in 1990, school districts and other education agencies across the United States have developed a variety of styles of delivering AT services. These vary from an "expert model," where members of an AT team are the only ones in the agency empowered to make recommendations about the selection, acquisition, and use of AT, to "capacity building models," where the members of the AT team spend their time training and supporting members of the IEP teams and student services teams so that they can effectively perform those tasks as independently as possible.

A survey of 55 teams from 22 states (DeCoste, Reed, & Kaplan, 2005) found that the majority of AT teams have teachers, speech/language pathologists, and occupational therapists on them. About a quarter of those teams reported having an administrative or coordinator position for their AT team. Fewer AT teams (15% or less) reported having physical therapists, vision specialists, hearing specialists, and school psychologists/diagnosticians on their AT teams. Evaluation of students' needs, consultation to staff, and staff training were reported as their primary roles.

Common Questions about AT Services

What does an AT evaluation include?

AT evaluations must identify both devices and services designed to allow the child to increase the quality or quantity of their performance, or independence in the everyday activities identified by the IEP team. Simply identifying a device does not give the classroom staff enough information about what is required for successful use. Evaluations should be, at least in part, completed in customary environments. This includes schools, classrooms, and other places where the child needs to complete the task that is of concern. Unless some part of the assessment is done in the environment where the student will use it, there is no way to know how effective the AT will be. The assessment is incomplete without those data, and the school district has not yet complied with the mandate. When a school uses an outside evaluator for AT assessment, the school-based team can still ensure that at least part of the evaluation is completed in the customary environment. To accomplish this, the team might take the recommendation from the outside evaluator and conduct functional trials in the settings where the AT will be used. Only after those trials would a decision about permanent acquisition and long-term use be made.

What sources of funding may be used to purchase AT?

Funding the purchase of AT is often an issue if an expensive device is needed. School districts are required to provide the needed AT but may seek outside funding or other assistance with the purchase. Both Judge (2000) and the National Task Force on Technology and Disability (2004) found that a lack of funding was one of the major barriers to making needed AT available. Dell, Newton, and Petroff (2008) point out that one of the primary causes of the substantial gap between the possibilities of AT for students with disabilities and actual implementation in our schools is the lack of funding. When combined with the misconception that all AT is expensive, it creates a large barrier to the provision of AT to students with disabilities.

However, the use of district/agency funds is not required in IDEA if other funding is available. The primary sources of funding for AT for children in addition to school district special education budgets include medical assistance/Medicaid and private insurance. Generally, Medicaid will purchase, rent, or lease some types of AT for children who are Medicaid beneficiaries. Parents can be asked, but not be required, to help purchase AT through the use of insurance or other funding sources.

Access to the needed AT cannot be delayed while funding is being sought. It is always best practice to borrow or rent the designated device or provide a reasonable facsimile so that the child can be making progress on IEP goals while funding for a permanent device is being obtained. For example, if a student needs a complicated communication device that will take several weeks to order, the district could begin training the student to use the device by using computer software or an app that emulates it. The student is then acquiring needed skills while waiting for the AT to arrive.

What is the education agency's responsibility to repair and maintain AT?

If AT is needed, it must be available and working at all times. If a school district is meeting its obligation to provide AT by using a device that belongs to the family, then it may need to repair that device if it is damaged or provide a replacement for use at school to ensure that the AT is available to implement the IEP. IEP teams also should have a backup plan for times when a device is out of service. Such a plan might include where to borrow or rent another device or how to set up a laptop computer to temporarily serve as a communication device during the repair period.

What does it mean to coordinate AT with other services?

Without good planning and coordination, AT is unlikely to be integrated into customary environments or functional activities. AT used only in isolation is ineffective. Real use in meaningful activities is the only way that AT can increase or improve a child's function. Because it must be used in the classroom and other settings on a regular basis, only the individuals who work in the classroom on a daily basis can make sure that a child has these critical daily opportunities to use the technology in real-life situations. In order to do this, staff members (teacher and classroom assistants) must have a thorough understanding of the technology. If there is a person on the team who has primary responsibility for providing AT services, that person can coordinate services by acting in a consultative role to other staff members, helping them to integrate use of the AT in a meaningful way.

When students have complex disabilities, a number of service providers may contribute to the educational program. Students may have an occupational therapist, physical therapist, speech and language pathologist, educational consultant, and vision or hearing specialist on their team. If AT is to be an effective tool for a child, all team members must have a clear understanding of the role the AT will play for the individual and their part in ensuring the success of the program.

What kinds of training and technical assistance are needed for the child and family?

The student needs training in both the operation of the device and in the functional area for which the device is identified. For example, a student who will use a computer for writing needs to know how the computer and the associated software work, and also needs instruction in the mechanics of writing sentences and paragraphs (the amount and type of instruction needed may or may not be the same for all students). Family members need to know what the child is doing and how AT use is expected to impact performance in all customary environments. If the family doesn't understand, can't support, or has unrealistic expectations for what the AT will do, its use will be much less successful.

What training and technical assistance is needed by professionals?

Because many service providers do not receive training in the operation and use of AT in their preservice programs (Hasselbring & Glaser, 2000), and because new technology is continually being developed, there is an ongoing need for training and technical assistance. Lack of training for professional staff leads to under use, inappropriate use, and—finally—abandonment of the AT (Scherer, 2000). The training needs of all members of the student's team should be assessed so that training can be provided to meet those needs. Typical training needs include awareness training about the range of AT available to address specific needs, in-depth training on specific hardware or software that the staff will be expected to use, training on how to evaluate the effectiveness of AT being used, and information on how and when to seek technical assistance. Effective training for professionals ensures that the plans made by the IEP team can be implemented and that the student will have the opportunity to learn to use AT to overcome barriers posed by the disability.

Documenting AT in the IEP

A student's IEP is the document that ensures that she will receive the services needed to benefit from the educational program and make progress in the curriculum. It is the document that will accompany that student after a transition to new schools and environments or a move to a different district. If AT is provided in a setting but is not documented in the IEP, it will most likely not be provided in the new setting. When this happens, the educators start over, trying to figure out how this student can achieve goals and make the necessary progress. There is nothing more wasteful or expensive than constantly starting over. The most expensive AT device is the one sitting unused on the shelf, because the money spent to purchase it was wasted, the salary spent on the person who taught the student to use it was wasted, and now the salary spent on the person starting from scratch is being wasted. We don't have money to waste in education. We need to get it right and document in the IEP what works.

IDEA includes the requirement that each IEP team consider a child's need for AT. It is one of five special factors included in IDEA. While the first four special factors refer to very specific areas of need or disability, the last one, which addresses AT consideration, has no such limitation. Rather, every IEP team must consider whether the child needs AT devices and services. Although most education agencies have a question about AT on the IEP form in order to comply with federal law, it is often not well understood by the IEP team members and not used effectively. The law reads as follows:

Consideration of special factors. The IEP Team shall

(i) In the case of a child whose behavior impedes the child's learning or that of others, consider the use of positive behavioral interventions and supports, and other strategies, to address that behavior;

(ii) In the case of a child with limited English proficiency, consider the language needs of the child as those needs relate to the child's IEP;

(iii) In the case of a child who is blind or visually impaired, provide for instruction in Braille and the use of Braille unless the IEP Team determines, after an evaluation of the child's reading and writing skills, needs, and appropriate reading and writing media (including an evaluation of the child's future needs for instruction in Braille or the use of Braille), that instruction in Braille or the use of Braille is not appropriate for the child;

(iv) Consider the communication needs of the child, and in the case of a child who is deaf or hard of hearing, consider the child's language and communication needs, opportunities for direct communications with peers and professional personnel in the child's language and communication mode, academic level, and full range of needs, including opportunities for direct instruction in the child's language and communication mode; and

(v) **Consider whether the child needs assistive technology devices and services.**

(emphasis added) Authority: IDEA Sec. 614(d)(3)(B)

Unfortunately, IEP teams often have a difficult time effectively considering a student's need for AT unless they have had sufficient training to understand AT and what it does. A survey of educators about their understanding of AT (Ashton, Lee, and Vega, 2005) found that respondents who had 40 or more hours of training about AT felt that it was essential to students' daily routine and felt comfortable in identifying and using AT to ensure educational access. Respondents without training felt that AT was not important to students' daily activities and stated that they were not confident in identifying and using AT. In that same study, nearly 90% of the respondents stated that their preservice preparation programs did not adequately emphasize AT use.

Assistive Technology: Make It Part of School Improvement

Assistive technology is an important part of the tools and strategies available to educators as they strive to provide an effective education for students with disabilities. It is most effective when AT is part of a comprehensive, well-designed program that includes other technology-based interventions. Universal Design for Learning (UDL) and accessible educational materials (AEM) are two concepts included in federal law that work together with AT to help students with special needs. It is important to recognize the symbiotic relationship between UDL, AEM, and AT. UDL is a practice of adapting the curriculum at the planning stage to consider the widest possible range of learners so that all instructional activities provide multiple means of

- accessing information,

- staying engaged in the learning process, and

- demonstrating (expressing) knowledge gained.

UDL was included in No Child Left Behind 2001 and IDEA 2004 with the goal of bringing general education and special education closer together. In a classroom using UDL, all students have access to a variety of technologies and accessibility features. Many school districts across the United States are implementing UDL at multiple grade levels. When UDL is in place, a student with a disability may find that the barriers he experienced in previous settings are removed. The student who acquires meaning from text more easily by listening to it can choose a variety of text-to-speech options; a student who better demonstrates what he has learned from a chapter by creating an audiovisual depiction can create a short video about the key concepts. If at some time in the future every classroom in every school district utilizes UDL principles, there will be less need to identify and use AT. However, until that time, IEP teams must use performance data to identify these accessibility features that are removing barriers to learning for students with disabilities and document them in the IEP as part of AT consideration.

IDEA (Section 300.172) requires that states and districts provide accessible educational materials (AEM) to students who are unable to utilize print-based materials, whether due to blindness or another print disability. It created the National Instructional Materials Access Center (NIMAC), a federally funded electronic file repository to receive and distribute specialized files that meet a standard for accessibility, the National Instructional Materials Accessibility Standard (NIMAS). The NIMAS files are received by the NIMAC and then distributed to states to be converted into specialized formats for student who are blind or have another print disability. The NIMAS source files come from textbook publishers but are not ready for use by school districts. Each state identifies authorized users who can convert the NIMAS files into Braille, audio, large print, or digital text formats and distribute the accessible versions to eligible students.

Students receiving AEM often need AT in order to access and use the materials. In that case, the AEM and AT work together to allow the student to access instruction, meet IEP goals, and/or make progress in the curriculum. Teachers who are already incorporating one of these strategies into their instruction will find that including all three is actually easier.

All of these technology-based interventions are being used in general education classrooms. General education teachers therefore need to be trained in the application and use of technology, including AT. Numerous national entities provide suggestions and tools to improve every aspect from instruction and school climate to family engagement. It is likely that your school program, building, and or agency are already engaged in a school improvement effort.

The effective provision of AT can be part of that school improvement effort. It can be folded into already existing programs where the goal is to improve graduation rates and postsecondary education enrollment. This book contains ideas for making AT part of that effort. It provides tools for self-assessment and suggestions for specific steps to take to improve outcomes for students with disabilities through the effective provision of AT.

CHAPTER 2

Leadership for AT Services

Use this chapter to create a shared vision for the assistive technology services that your program provides.

- ✔ Know who the AT leaders are in the agency and work with them directly to develop, maintain, and improve AT services.

- ✔ Help staff, students, and families develop a vision for AT use and communicate that vision widely.

- ✔ Support faculty and staff in using AT to improve the education of students with disabilities.

- ✔ Develop a culture where AT devices and services are valued and used.

- ✔ Facilitate and support collaboration between departments to improve learning for students with disabilities through the use of AT.

Leadership is a process of motivating and helping any group to achieve its goals. Leadership in schools impacts the motivation and commitment of teachers, increases their capacity to change their practices, and alters their working conditions (Leithwood, Harris, & Hopkins, 2008). Leadership is critical to the field of assistive technology, and school administrators play an important role in providing that leadership. No matter what tasks an administrator is engaged in, it is the complex issues that most urgently require leadership. Administrators and AT leaders encourage appropriate actions from others, set the tone for future actions, and create a vehicle to identify solutions to systemic AT questions.

Assistive technology services include not only those services provided by staff with AT expertise or AT in their job description, but also those services to support student use of AT that are provided by classroom teachers, educational assistants, related service providers, and anyone else who supports the student's learning and growth. The provision of AT may raise many complex issues that require school administrators to play an active role in addressing them. This chapter will focus on the role of the school administrator as a leader in AT services.

Assigned Leaders and Emergent Leaders

Some individuals are leaders because of the assigned administrative position that they fill (e.g., school principal, special education director). Other individuals may become leaders in changing AT services because of their knowledge of AT devices and services or the way others in the group respond to them. Northouse (2016) labels these two types of leaders as *assigned leaders* and *emergent leaders.* In their survey of established AT teams, DeCoste, Reed, and Kaplan (2005) found that only 20% of the teams surveyed stated that assigned leaders (i.e., administrators) initiated their AT team development. More commonly, AT team activities were developed as enthusiastic direct service providers saw a need for AT coordination. Yet without administrative support, AT improvement efforts are likely to be less effective and more difficult to sustain. In changing the nature or style of AT service provision, assigned administrators and AT leaders can be extremely effective working together to lead change.

Assigned leaders are individuals such as special education administrators or building principals. They have the ability and responsibility to assign staff to specific roles, teams, and tasks; coordinate with other departments; and advocate for funding. Because of their assigned position, school administrators have authority to lead change. Although they may not always be familiar with specific AT content, their assignment gives them the responsibility to make sure that a high-quality AT program is provided.

JOE'S STORY: THE ASSIGNED LEADER

When Joe became Director of Student Services for a small rural school district, he had very little experience with AT. Despite this fact, he felt confident, because the district employed an occupational therapist (OT) who was assigned to support AT use for all students in the district as half of his job responsibilities. Joe had been told by his predecessor that there were many students using AT in each of the district's 15 schools, so he was pretty sure that this was a service area that was well addressed in the district.

Joe met with each staff member as he took on his new job responsibilities, and the OT assigned to AT services was one of those people. He reported that, though the district had operating guidelines and procedures for most AT services, there appeared to be concerns about integration of AT into daily routines and activities for some students. Together, they wondered how they could get more information about the quality of the district's AT services.

Joe, in his role as assigned administrator, and the OT, in her role as AT leader, decided to use the Education Tech Points: Profile of AT Services in Schools (see Appendix A) as a tool for evaluating how things were going in the district. Joe was able to ask every special education teacher and every related service provider to complete the self-evaluation for his or her position.

The AT leader was able to re-create the self-evaluation in an electronic form so that when each special education professional entered the information, the data could be aggregated with other responses and sorted by age group, disability category served, type of classroom, and type of related service. The data that Joe and the AT leader collected indicated that students who used AT successfully in elementary school were less successful with their AT use at the middle schools and that middle school educators reported a lower level of AT service than did those at the elementary schools.

After collecting this information, Joe and his AT leader made a plan of action. Joe's approach was to begin to work with all principals in the district to help them with ideas about how to monitor AT use in their schools. The district's AT leader began to focus on further assessment of the services provided at the middle school level in order to identify actions to improve continuity of AT use for students who made a transition from elementary to middle school.

Emergent leaders in AT are those who have an AT background and may be direct AT service providers. AT leaders usually come to their leadership naturally because of their enthusiasm for the work. They are recognized by others for their passion about AT's benefits for students with disabilities or as experts in AT. Emergent leaders often have specific information that allows them to explain AT to others, train staff members on key AT tools and strategies, share information about new and emerging technologies, and see the need for changes that can more effectively meet students' needs.

AT programs experience the most benefit when administrators work closely with AT leaders to make changes that will improve the overall AT program. Leithwood et al. (2008) found that there is no loss of administrative influence in a school when the power and influence of many others in the school is increased and used. In fact, staff in schools with the highest levels of student achievement attributed their success to influence from multiple sources of leadership (Mascall & Leithwood, 2008). School administrators know a great deal about how to make the system work and are assigned to initiate actions that lead to change. AT leaders generally understand more about specific aspects of a desired change in AT services and have much to contribute in leading everyone involved to implement consistent aspects of the new approach.

Depending on the background of the administrator, she may need a lot of information from the AT leader or not much at all. On occasion, these two roles may be embodied in the same individual, who is an administrator with a passion for improving AT services or who has a background as an AT service provider. When the administrator has little or no background in AT and the desired outcome is a major change, AT leaders are essential collaborators. At the same time, AT leaders who have little or no experience in administration may not have the background or experience to know what kind of resources they need or the actions to undertake to make change. Administrators and AT leaders balance each other's contributions. Together they can be a powerful team.

It is also important to be clear about the limits to a school administrator's role in AT. Rarely are school administrators AT experts who can provide direct AT services or make independent AT decisions. Instead, administrators lead by developing the context in which those tasks will be carried out. In AT, as well as all aspects of school operation, the successful administrator

- helps teachers recognize the need for change when appropriate (Zimmerman, 2006; Greenberg & Baron, 2000),

- takes the lead in developing a vision and mission (Bateman & Bateman, 2001),

- recognizes and utilizes other's expertise (Parsons, 2001),

- leads by example (Technology Standards for School Administrators, 2001),

- keeps in touch with the students who use AT (Murphy & Lick, 2001), and

- develops a climate of inquiry and continuous self-improvement (Blase & Blase, 2001; Brewer, 2001).

Zimmerman (2006) cites these steps found in the leadership and organizational change literature as key to making successful change:

1. create a sense of urgency,

2. develop and operationalize a vision,

3. reward constructive behaviors, and

4. aim for short-term successes.

Leaders can create this sense of urgency in their schools by sharing data with teachers about their students' test results relative to the state report card levels and focusing on ways to close the achievement gaps for all groups, including struggling students and students with disabilities. The purpose of this is not to unnecessarily pressure teachers with data, but rather to help them look at ways to improve that data, including the use of AT by students with disabilities.

Creating a professional learning community is one strategy to help teachers work together to manage their learning and plan constructive change (Zimmerman, 2006). It provides a vehicle to focus on critical issues as they work to improve students' performance.

As educators at the secondary level began to address the inconsistencies they had found in elementary and secondary AT services, they called on the OT more and more for consultation and technical assistance. The teachers in one middle school determined that more than half of their students needed to begin to learn text-to-speech options embedded in the school's software suite and that most of them would need at least one textbook in a format that could be read aloud. This was seen as a great success. But it also created new issues and problems for the OT because she was the only identified person in the district who knew text to speech and who could provide electronic versions of textbooks.

Joe and the OT decided to create a "community of practice" group whose members could be called on to support each other in the uses of text to speech and accessible educational materials (AEM). This group took on some of the responsibilities that the OT had been carrying, which left her free to deal with file and software acquisition and installation. Previously, educators had called on the OT for all of these functions, but based on district resources and the results of the Education Tech Points: Profile of AT Services in Schools (Reed and Bowser, 2017), they decided to build the capacity of community of practice members to take independent action and support each other as a more effective and sustainable option. They acknowledged that the OT would always be available to support community members and provide additional expertise when needed.

Quality Indicators for Assistive Technology

One of many barriers to both individual and organizational change that has been documented in the literature is a failure to recognize the need for change (Greenberg & Baron, 2000). Unless teachers understand and appreciate the need for change in their schools, their interest in maintaining the status quo will undoubtedly take precedence over their willingness to accept change (Greenberg & Baron, 2000).

Educators who wish to make a change and help their colleagues along should consult the Quality Indicators for Assistive Technology (QIAT—see Appendix B). The Indicators are a national consensus of what best indicates accomplished AT service provision in schools. The Quality Indicators are a series of descriptors of critical components of AT services. They were developed over several years with input from more than 4,000 service providers, family members, and users of AT across the United States (QIAT Leadership Team, 2015). Their perceived importance, validity, and utility are supported by a study by Zabala (2007). The eight Quality Indicator areas are:

- Consideration of Assistive Technology Needs: Consideration of the need for AT devices and services is an integral part of the educational process contained in IDEA for referral, evaluation, and IEP development. Although

AT is considered at all stages of the process, the Consideration Quality Indicators are specific to the consideration of AT in the development of the IEP as mandated by the Individuals with Disabilities Education Act (IDEA). In most instances, the Quality Indicators are also appropriate for the consideration of AT for students who qualify for services under other legislation (e.g., 504, ADA).

- Assessment of Assistive Technology Needs: Applying the Quality Indicators for Assessment of Assistive Technology Needs is a process, conducted by a team, used to identify tools and strategies to address a student's specific needs. The issues that lead to an AT assessment may be simple and quickly answered or more complex and challenging. Assessment takes place when these issues are beyond the scope of the problem solving that occurs as a part of normal service delivery.

- Including AT in the IEP: The Individuals with Disabilities Education Improvement Act (IDEA) requires that the IEP team consider AT needs in the development of every Individualized Education Program (IEP). Once the IEP team has reviewed assessment results and determined that AT is needed for provision of a free appropriate public education (FAPE), it's important that the IEP document reflects the team's determination as clearly as possible. The Quality Indicators for AT in the IEP help the team describe the role of AT in the child's educational program.

- Implementation: Assistive technology implementation pertains to the ways that assistive technology devices and services, as included in the IEP (including goals/objectives, related services, supplementary aids and services, and accommodations or modifications) are delivered and integrated into the student's educational program. Assistive technology implementation involves people working together to support the student using AT to accomplish expected tasks necessary for active participation and progress in customary educational environments.

- Evaluation of Effectiveness of AT: This area addresses the evaluation of the effectiveness of the AT devices and services that are provided to individual students. It includes data collection, documentation, and analysis to monitor changes in student performance resulting from the implementation of assistive technology services. Student performance is reviewed in order to identify if, when, or where modifications and revisions to the implementation are needed.

- Assistive Technology Transition: Transition plans for students who use assistive technology address the ways the students' use of assistive technology devices and services is transferred from one setting to another. Assistive technology transition involves people from different classrooms, programs, buildings, or agencies working together to ensure continuity.

Self-determination, advocacy, and implementation are critical issues for transition planning.

- Professional Development and Training in AT: This area defines the critical elements of quality professional development and training in assistive technology. Assistive technology professional development and training efforts should arise out of an ongoing, well-defined, sequential, and comprehensive plan.

- Administrative Support of Assistive Technology Services: This area defines the critical areas of administrative support and leadership for developing and delivering assistive technology services. It involves the development of policies, procedures, and other supports necessary to improve quality of services and sustain effective assistive technology programs.

The Quality Indicators support systematic decision-making and implementation in all aspects of AT service delivery as well as guidance for effectively documenting, organizing, and monitoring AT selection, acquisition, and use by individual students. The particular areas align to specific areas of responsibility in special-education processes that may require services to support the use of AT.

For a handbook on how to implement them, see the book *Quality Indicators for Assistive Technology: A Comprehensive Guide to Assistive Technology Services* (2015), published by CAST Professional Publishing (*www.castpublishing.org*), or go online at *www.qiat.org*.

Developing a Vision for AT Services

One of the most important leadership roles in AT is helping stakeholders develop a vision of what AT services should be in their setting. When leaders include teachers and other stakeholders in developing a shared vision and goals for reaching the vision, their actions give meaning, a common purpose, challenge, and motivation to everyone involved (Bass & Avolio, 1994; Marzano, Waters, & McNulty, 2005; Schmoker, 1999; Senge, Kleiner, Roberts, Ross, Roth, & Smith, 1999). Administrators can bring those stakeholders together to enable them to develop a shared vision of how AT can play a role in enhancing student achievement. Focusing on the ways that AT contributes to student performance can help develop a shared vision of AT's contribution to school improvement. AT does not have to be viewed as a separate issue for individual students but can be folded into overall school efforts. Just as the full use of instructional technology by teachers and students is achieved only through the support and vision of a technology-savvy administrator (Technology Standards for School Administrators Collaborative, 2001), the full use of AT is achieved only with that same support and vision.

An AT leader can provide specific information and examples that help shape the vision, thus complementing the administrator's role in promoting overall student achievement by creating a vision, mission, and goals for the school or district. Because students with disabilities are included in many general education classrooms, all educators—not just special education staff—must understand AT and share a vision for its use. It is this shared vision that creates the environment and context that allows the development of effective services. If there is no shared vision, and if the culture does not support or encourage student use of AT, individual AT specialists trying to coach teachers or assistants to implement the use of AT struggle against often insurmountable barriers.

Before beginning a visioning process, everyone involved needs to have a sense of what high-quality AT services look like.

Components of an AT Vision

In preparing to develop a vision for the agency, administrators and AT leaders might develop a set of questions such as the following to gather information and data about the state of AT services:

Questions about students' use of AT:

Which students currently use AT?

What types of AT do they use?

What percentage of students with disabilities have AT?

Are there students who could benefit from AT but haven't had it made available?

Questions about staff members' knowledge about and use of AT:

Do teachers know what AT is available?

Do they know how to request it?

Do teachers or other staff need training about AT to be active participants in AT consideration during the IEP?

Do they need training to use AT in their practice?

Questions about agency or district resources:

Where might training be obtained?

Is there an AT team?

Is there a need to develop an AT team?

If an AT team is required, what role should that team play (i.e., should members directly assess students and make recommendations, or should they focus on building the capacity of all teachers, therapists, and assistants to provide these services)?

These questions can begin to provide a picture of the use of AT and the knowledge base about it. Paired with the results of the Education Tech Points: Profile of AT Services in Schools (Bowser & Reed, 2017), this information can help focus the discussion on developing a vision.

Whether there will be an AT team, and what that team will do, is an important component of the vision of AT services. The primary decision to be made is whether that team will use an expert model or a capacity-building model. That decision will determine many other components of the vision.

If the agency currently has an AT team or has the development of an AT team in the vision for their AT services, the administrator and AT leader can work together to plan for and support that team. Things to consider include (a) the skill sets that need to be represented (e.g., knowledge about language development, knowledge about seating and positioning, knowledge about technology for reading and writing, and knowledge about curricular demands in the district); (b) the specific individuals in the agency who have that knowledge; (c) how much FTE the agency will allocate for an AT team; (d) available facilities (e.g., office space, desks, and computers); (e) budget for AT (both personnel and equipment); and (f) available storage for AT devices when not assigned to individual students. Decisions like these will be addressed in subsequent chapters about management, supervision, and program improvement.

As part of ongoing efforts for school improvement, an administrator also may encourage new individuals to take a leadership role in helping others learn more about AT. As a leader of leaders, the administrator has a powerful effect on the performance of the staff (Ash & Persall, 2000). An administrator might encourage a task force to analyze student data and investigate the impact of AT use across classes and grades. Assigning responsibility for this type of investigation enhances and encourages not only the learning of students, but also the learning of the adults working with those students.

AT leaders can research and share information about existing models of AT service delivery and the ways that the models match the vision and resources of the agency. They can provide information to administrators in order to help them be aware of and commend exemplary AT use throughout the agency.

Using Agency Expertise

One of the most important aspects of developing a shared vision of AT services is helping both special education teachers and general classroom teachers recognize the important roles they play in successful AT use. Classroom teachers are the only school professionals who can identify opportunities for the student to use AT in a meaningful and productive way and ensure that these opportunities are available on a daily basis. No therapist who provides itinerant services or consultation and no AT specialist who serves as a resource can provide these critical opportunities for technology use.

When teacher capacity to provide AT services is part of the agency vision, administrators can take action to help build that capacity. Training and professional development is usually provided as part of supervision activities. Management activities such as the development of written procedural guidelines may emphasize the role that each educator takes in AT services. However, the need for these kinds of administrative actions becomes apparent only when a clear vision exists of the way the agency thinks about the services provided. An agency that focuses on building the capacity of educators to independently provide AT services will use its resources much differently than an agency that has a one-to-one expert consultant model of AT services.

Valuing AT Use

People perform differently in different contexts. When AT use is widespread and visible throughout a school, teachers will be encouraged to expand their use of AT. Administrators who are knowledgeable about the specific students who use AT and the role various educators play in supporting that use establish expectations that AT is important in the school environment. When administrators ask questions of educators about technology use, educators' attention to the technology is heightened (Blase & Blase, 2001). Just asking about a student's technology use can be an important AT leadership activity.

AT leaders can help administrators create a culture that values AT by making sure that they have specific information about the AT that students use, the ways that the AT helps students function more independently, and the kinds of things to look for when completing formal and informal observations.

Supporting AT Use

Administrators set the tone for desirable behaviors in the school. They do this through modeling, formal recognition of staff and students, and informal conversation and comments. Administrators who value the use of AT demonstrate those values every day in many small ways. They might congratulate a teacher who has just mastered the use of new software that will help students who are struggling with reading, stop and converse with a student who uses a voice output communication device, or encourage a student who is working hard to operate a power wheelchair independently. AT leaders can help administrators support AT use by alerting them to successes and new ideas that should be highlighted.

Another form of support includes recognition throughout the school of students who use their AT in particularly effective ways. For example, a middle school student who creates a video report rather than writing a paper might receive special recognition for the quality of the alternative strategy. A student who gives a speech to her class about her summer trip to Harry Potter World using her augmentative and alternative communication (AAC) device might be asked to post a recording of her speech on the classroom or school web page so that everyone could hear it.

When a school administrator encourages discussion and reflection on a topic, it promotes growth and improves teaching (Blase & Blase, 2001). If increasing the academic performance of all students is a goal, the administrator can encourage staff members to share ideas, including the use of AT, at every staff meeting. He will also make it a point to inquire about whether or not students have their AT available in all academic settings. This communicates the message that the administrator considers AT availability an important goal for which everyone has a responsibility.

Leadership: Getting Started

This chapter talked about the many ways that administrators and AT leaders can impact AT services through leadership activities. The following are some specific suggestions for getting started.

Actions for Administrators

- Assess your AT services using the Education Tech Points: Profile of AT Services in Schools and review the results.

- Make a list of the questions you have about AT use in your building or program.

- Identify three opportunities that you typically have where advocating for AT use might be appropriate and effective.

- Identify barriers to collaboration with other parts of the agency and initiate outreach efforts to those groups.

Actions for AT Leaders

- Report regularly to your administrator about your service model and the ways that you approach the provision of direct AT services, professional development, outreach to other parts of the agency, and your long-term plans to build capacity.

- Collect, analyze, and share data about the activities of staff members engaged in supporting educators and families to use AT.

- Discuss goals and activities with your administrator with the intention of identifying specific ways that you can support each other in leading AT services in your district.

- Help your administrator identify places within the educational system where collaboration with other departments or other parts of the agency may be needed. Suggest outreach activities that may encourage that collaboration.

CHAPTER 3

Management for AT Services

Use this chapter to identify internal processes and operating guidelines to help you create productive working environments and ensure that assistive technology services are legal, efficient, equitable, and cost-effective.

- ✔ Ensure equity of access to AT devices and services for students of all ages, disabilities, and school placements.

- ✔ Develop, implement, and monitor procedures and written operating guidelines for providing AT services that include processes for AT consideration and documentation, AT assessment, and implementation of AT plans.

- ✔ Ensure that all appropriate employees know how to respond to a parent's request for AT.

- ✔ Require that staff use data to make AT decisions.

- ✔ Make funds, human resources, and planning time available for the provision of AT services.

- ✔ Upgrade the AT inventory as needed.

- ✔ Monitor AT services to ensure they are provided in a cost-effective and efficient manner.

Productive schools exhibit a high degree of consistency where staff members use well-understood policies to guide the daily operation. Members of a well-managed organization should expect that routine matters will be dealt with in fair and consistent ways so that the other aspects can be addressed to improve the performance of all students. (Uben & Hughes, 1997)

The job of providing staff with the stability and conditions needed to do effective work falls largely to school administrators. School leaders keep the whole program on an even keel so that staff members understand daily goals and expectations. Effective school leaders also help facilitate positive interpersonal interactions. Day-to-day management takes up an enormous amount of time and often includes tasks that may feel repetitive and tedious to a creative administrator. Scheduling fire drills, making sure the furnace works, and signing contracts can frustrate a creative leader. However, these tasks are necessary to ensure productive working conditions for educators (Leithwood, Harris, & Hopkins, 2008).

Attending to how AT is provided is also an essential part of school leadership. School administrators and AT leaders need to work closely with AT teams to (a) ensure that AT services are effective and responsive to the needs of students and families; (b) allocate the physical, human, and monetary resources needed to provide AT devices and services; and (c) ensure accountability so that AT services are equitable, efficient, ethical, legal, and cost-effective. Working with teams, the administrator can ensure the development of effective processes and systems to make sure the law is followed and that students have the resources they need to succeed in learning.

Working with AT Leaders to Develop Processes and Systems

Without guidance, individual educators will arrive at a variety of unique and possibly diverse ways to take action when AT is involved. This can lead to problems for the school district as a result of inconsistency and unequal treatment. Administrators, in their role as program managers, can prevent difficult situations through the development of procedures and operating guidelines for AT services that will guide the actions of individual staff members and teams. IEP teams need a way of approaching AT that can apply to every student. If each student's team uses a different decision-making process, the agency's AT services will be inconsistent. Inconsistencies can create problems of equity across classrooms, grade levels, and programs and leave the agency vulnerable to complaints and due process hearings. The procedures an agency develops help its teams make decisions in a consistent and equitable way. They also provide the necessary degree of stability to ensure that AT services are effective and run smoothly.

An administrator does not have to know a lot about AT to take an important role in the development of AT operating guidelines. Administrators need to understand what AT is, the district's responsibility to provide it, and the limits of that responsibility.

Chapter 1, "Understanding Assistive Technology," describes the expectations of IDEA. Armed with this basic information and with help from AT leaders in the agency, an administrator, in the role of manager, can begin to develop answers to many of the procedural questions that arise for every child who might need AT. Administrators can call on AT leaders for help with understanding any issues or concepts that are unclear and to share additional information about the way that questions like these are addressed by other AT programs.

Operating guidelines and policies identify the actions that people should take in response to predictable and recurring events. Operating guidelines delegate specific tasks to team members and help to clarify roles. When educational agencies have operating guidelines, administrators' time is more available to handle unusual or unpredictable problems that may require individual attention (Uben & Hughes, 1997; Leithwood et al., 2008). In addition, a school's operating guidelines help staff, families, and students avoid disruption and confusion in implementing a child's educational program (Bowser, 2003).

Operating guidelines also make it less likely that there will be conflict about AT decisions and implementation. When every member of an IEP or Individualized Family Service Plan (IFSP) team has a clear picture of what will be done for a student, as well as how and when it will be done, it is easier to track progress, identify implementation strategies, and make sure they are put in place.

Written operating guidelines and policies address questions that must be answered at the program level. To be useful and effective, AT procedures must have a good fit with local resources and local practices. The guidelines don't have to be complicated or separate from other procedures and processes. In fact, it is helpful to everyone involved if they are an integrated part of day-to-day program operation.

Education Tech Points: A Framework for Assistive Technology (Bowser & Reed, 1995, 1998, 2012) identified key points in the special education delivery process where AT needs should be addressed. These "tech points" include referral, evaluation, consideration, IEP development, implementation, and transition. At each Education Tech Point, suggested questions the team should ask, actions the team should take, and implications for school districts can help to guide individual team process.

Aspects of AT Services to Be Addressed in Guidelines

Most of the issues that administrators and AT leaders will address through written guidelines center on initiating and responding to requests for AT. Others relate to decision making and documenting those decisions.

Under IDEA, educational agencies must have a process for addressing the educational needs of children with disabilities in all areas. Educators need to know how the agency's process applies to questions about the need for AT. By law, AT must be considered for every student who has an IEP. Guidelines can address what educators need to do when they believe a child needs AT. For example, if a team wants to try accessible instructional materials or AT tools, they need to know whether to initiate a formal referral and evaluation process or if they can try tools without the help of a specialist. Teachers also need to know

- what to do before initiating a request for support or for evaluation (i.e., pre-referral strategies),

- what data should accompany a referral or request for support,

- whether the agency's processes are different for children with mild disabilities than they are for children with more severe disabilities, and

- whether the assessment process is different for commonly available technology than it is for more specialized AT, such as augmentative communication devices.

Specific AT Requests

When a parent or other advocate formally requests an AT assessment, educators must know how to address the request in a legal and timely manner. An initial request for an AT assessment is similar to other requests for services, such as speech therapy or transportation, and AT requests can generally be treated in the same way. Everyone on the IEP team needs to know what forms to complete, who to send them to, how legal assessment timelines are applied, and what will happen after the assessment is initiated. A responsive process at this stage sets a tone that indicates that AT is an important topic that will be addressed in a complete and professional way. Guidelines that address these specific steps help ensure that parental requests will be responded to in a consistent manner across the agency.

When a parent asks for a trial of a specific AT device during an IEP meeting, one thing is certain: failure to respond can lead to dissatisfaction, disagreements, and even formal complaints to the state. An initial request for an AT assessment is similar to other requests for assessment or evaluation, and these requests should receive the same careful attention.

Parents sometimes ask for AT during informal conversations. Helping staff members know how to handle informal requests for AT devices or services can create an environment that is responsive to the concerns of parents and the needs of their children with disabilities. Even if the request is not presented in writing or during an official IEP meeting, educators need guidance about how to proceed. They need to know who else should be notified, how and when the request is to be documented (e.g., in contact notes, by filling out a specific form), and at what point in the conversation they should ask that the parent complete a permission-to-evaluate form. Written guidance about requests for AT can help team members to know

- how they can help parents reframe the question to identify the problem the child is experiencing;

- at what point a referral, permission-to-evaluate, or request-for-support form will need to be completed; and

- when parents request a specific AT device, whether that device should be identified on the referral or permission-to-evaluate form.

AT Assessment Processes

Because commonly used classroom tools can function as AT for many children with disabilities, a child's team may be able to assess AT need without outside help. Almost anyone can help a child try to use a calculator, a mobile tablet, or an electronic file that comes with a textbook. Educators can collect data about the effectiveness of such solutions, and an IEP team may be able to include them in an IEP without the help of a specialist. At the same time, if a team needs information about a particular kind of tool or if the AT needed by a child is complicated, outside help may be necessary.

Administrators and AT leaders can help teams understand what assistance is available in the district and who might provide the needed information. If an education agency does not have the kind of resources a team needs within the district, guidelines can identify outside resources that can be used. These might include education service agencies, the state education agency, or private centers or clinics. Once sources are identified, processes can also be established for internal and external referrals. Most education agencies have processes in place for using some outside assessment services, and the same process can be applied to AT assessment. Guidelines can include

- information resources available in the district,

- specific individuals who might provide AT information to an IEP team,

- outside resources that are available to IEP teams,

- the process to contact outside resources, and

- when and how administrators should be notified of the need for additional AT assessment.

Guidelines about Reporting and Communication

If individual educators or IEP teams are considering recommending a particular kind of AT for a child, they need to know how and when to notify supervisors and the information that will be required. Although administrators cannot make independent decisions that bypass the IEP consideration process established in IDEA, they can and should join team discussions when the team is considering unusual or high-cost recommendations. Sometimes a recommendation for high-cost AT comes from the IEP team. At other times, those recommendations may come from an outside source, such as a medical clinic or independent AT expert. Operating guidelines might identify when an administrator who does not normally attend an IEP meeting should be alerted to a potential recommendation for AT so that she can be present. Guidelines also might identify the source of funding for low-cost versus high-cost items and the process involved in acquiring them. The guidelines developed by each agency will depend, in part, on the way budgets are structured and funds are distributed for classroom materials. Specific guidelines related to the recommending of AT include

- whether administrators should be alerted if an AT recommendation will require only a small expenditure, and

- what to do if a device recommendation might cost a larger amount (e.g., more than $500).

Educators need to know what to do if there is conflict or disagreement about AT during the processes of assessment, consideration, or implementation. It is reasonable to expect that IEP teams will sometimes have difficulty coming to consensus about the needs of a particular child. Most education agencies have processes in place to help teams deal with conflict situations. Already established conflict resolution strategies can also be applied to AT. Specific guidelines about working through conflict during AT decision making include

- who needs to be notified when conflicts arise,

- under what circumstances an administrator should be informed about an AT disagreement among team members who are professionals, and

- under what circumstances an administrator should be informed that disagreement about AT exists between staff members and a parent team member.

Data-Based Decisions

Because IDEA requires that each IEP team consider the student's need for AT, many decisions about the need for AT will occur at that time. When considering AT, IEP teams need to know the kind of evidence they need to use to make a decision. Consideration of the need for AT is based on student academic and functional performance and assessment results. During consideration, the IEP team may realize that a student has failed to make progress on previous IEP goals, that the student's level of frustration is increasing, or that the student understands much more than he or she is able to demonstrate. These realizations should lead an IEP team to think about how AT could help this student.

Both general information about the student's past and present performance and specific data about that performance will be needed in order for the team to make a decision about the possible use of AT and to target the change in performance that might be expected through its use. If teams do not have information or data about the student's performance, it is preferable to make a plan to collect it, rather than to try to make a decision without any facts.

Trial periods are an essential part of any AT assessment. Before an IEP is written to include AT, educators must identify the anticipated outcome of AT use (i.e., the problem the AT will address) and, if at all possible, introduce the device to the child. This helps the IEP team to get an initial idea of the possible benefits the AT will provide. Trial periods are a little like test-driving a new car. The team needs to see how it might work for a child before committing to using it.

A student may have the opportunity to try AT without completing an entire AT assessment process. This might happen as part of a whole-class experience with technology or as a result of an informal trial with a specific AT tool. In this case, educators may have data about how the student performs both with and without the use of that technology. Evidence indicating a need for AT might include changes in the student's quality, quantity, or speed in the identified functional skill. Evidence-based decisions about AT are more likely to be equitable and result in effective use of the technology.

At the district level, administrators can help develop a description of the kinds of data that IEP teams should use when they consider AT, and AT leaders can help ensure that educators who serve as IEP team members are aware of the range of AT that exists and where to get more information about AT. Guidance about data-driven decision making includes

- how IEP teams can frame an initial, data-based AT question so that the role AT will play in helping the student to achieve educational goals can be determined,

- evidence teams will need to collect before recommending an AT solution, and

- how results of a trial period and recommendations are to be reported to the IEP team.

AT Documentation

Once the need for AT is identified, it is written into the IEP. Educators need guidance about how to write IEPs. Guidance about AT in IEPs will include the district's approach to developing specific functional goals and the listing of AT as accommodations or modifications. Specifics such as whether to include the specific brand name of hardware or software also will need to be addressed. It is usually recommended that the name of a specific product not be written into the IEP until that product has been shown to be successful for the student in customary environments. Specific guidelines about writing AT into the IEP include

- how and where the decision that a child needs AT can be documented, and

- whether devices in the IEP are described by their features. If it is ever acceptable to list the name of a specific AT device,

- under what circumstances a child would have specific goals for AT device use, and

- when the use of AT would be listed as an accommodation or supplemental aid.

AT in Other Settings

The district's policy about sending AT home with a student and what to do if it is damaged due to neglect is an important area to define. IDEA requires that AT must be provided at home if the child needs it to accomplish IEP goals. IDEA also says that states may make policies about what should happen if damage of the AT occurs due to neglect. Many states have deferred this policy-making responsibility to local education agencies. District loan policies for other expensive things like band instruments, athletic equipment, and scientific calculators can usually be applied to the loan of AT. Specific guidance about AT use and damage at home includes

- who to notify about damaged school-owned AT devices, and times when administrators need to be notified that AT has been damaged;

- how the team should proceed if AT is included on the IEP for home use and it is damaged;

- at what point the IEP should be modified if AT that is sent home is frequently damaged; and

- if a change in an IEP that includes AT used at home seems warranted, how the team should proceed.

DISTRICT-OWNED DEVICES AT HOME: AN EXAMPLE

Mid Central School District began developing guidelines for AT. The AT Committee included the middle school principal, the special education director, and the AT specialist/occupational therapist for the district. The three worked well together using their expertise and contacts to find the information needed.

When developing guidelines for providing AT for use at home, they wondered what should be included and what they could do to address school-owned AT that is sent home and damaged. The principal checked to see what the district policy was for band instruments that are sent home. The special education director researched what federal and state law said about the district's ability to charge families for damages if they occur, and the AT specialist checked with AT personnel in other districts to find out about their policies.

They learned quite a lot that helped shape their policy for AT use at home. They decided to require IEP teams to determine, on an individual basis, whether a student needed to be able to use AT tools at home in order to receive a free appropriate public education (FAPE). The special education director acquired a state guidance document showing that families should not have to pay for AT, though they could be held responsible financially for its loss or damage beyond normal wear and tear. They planned to include the requirement that families receive training on the device and its care, including charging, prior to sending any AT home. The AT committee also decided that their home-use policy needed to address these issues:

- how to determine who might need to use the AT at home,

- what modifications may be made to the AT by family members and other supporters,

- to whom problems and malfunctions with the device should be reported and when,

- what to do when the student forgets the device at home, and

- how replacement and repair is handled if the AT is not available at school and at home due to theft or damage due to negligence or misuse.

They planned to have the policy reviewed by the district's legal counsel and to ask a broader range of staff to review the guidelines to ensure that they made sense to the intended audience.

The district's policy about provision of AT to students in private schools also needs to be clearly laid out. To address IDEA mandates, school districts have developed guidelines regarding the provision of services to students with disabilities who attend private schools. The policy that the school district has developed regarding services in private schools should be applied to AT. Educators may need help with the specifics of how these policies are applied. Educators who work for education service agencies that serve multiple school districts need to know the policies of each school district they support since the policies may differ from agency to agency. Specific key points about AT provision in private schools include

- the overall district policy about provision of services to students with disabilities who attend private schools,

- whether it is acceptable for AT devices to be provided in the private school setting, and

- whether it is acceptable for AT services to be provided in the private school setting.

The following is an example of a district process that was provided to staff as part of operating guidelines.

Prior to the IEP Meeting

Each IEP team member should collect information about

- the student, the environments where the student experiences barriers to meeting IEP goals or accessing the curriculum, and the tasks the student needs to accomplish;

- the adaptations, accommodations, and AT options that have been tried to date to assist the student in overcoming barriers to learning; and

- school site resources and options that might help the student to overcome barriers to learning.

During the IEP Meeting

Team members should jointly

- describe the student's present level of educational performance;

- identify areas of concern;

- identify annual goals and short-term objectives;

- continue to recommend school-site AT resources and interventions until the student's needs are met, or until it is determined that school-site personnel lack the necessary expertise to make further recommendations; and

- document AT decisions made during the meeting.

STEPS FOR IEP TEAMS WHEN CONSIDERING AT NEEDS

When More Information Is Needed

Team members should jointly

- document the results of the AT consideration in the IEP or meeting minutes,

- obtain permission to further evaluate the child's need for assistive technology, and

- develop an assistive technology assessment plan.

After the IEP Meeting

Team members should

- arrange to obtain any needed assistive technology;

- develop an implementation plan that includes student training, staff training, device maintenance, and ongoing evaluation procedures and implement the plan, *or* initiate the planned assessment; and

- reconvene the IEP meeting to review progress and modify the program if necessary.

Once procedures and operating guidelines have been established, administrators and AT leaders ensure that everyone knows about them and how they are to be implemented. In order to be effective, operating guidelines must be widely disseminated and readily available to teams when a question arises.

The operating guidelines that an educational agency develops help to ensure that services are efficient, ethical, legal, and cost-effective. They also help to shape management decisions about allocation of money, time, and personnel.

Working with AT Leaders to Allocate Resources for AT Devices and Services

In their role as managers, administrators develop budgets, allocate resources to specific programs and activities, and ensure that all educators have, to the greatest extent possible, the tools and physical resources they need to do their part in the education of students. Supporting AT use includes tackling the *TEARS*. The TEARS are the issues that have been identified for more than 70 years as roadblocks to using technology (Cuban, 1986; Leggett & Persichitte, 1998). They are

Time

Expertise

Access

Resources

Support

These five obstacles were first identified when teachers were asked to learn to use movie projectors. They arise every time new technology is introduced in classrooms, and each aspect of TEARS must be addressed in order for technology to be effectively used in schools.

Time

Personnel who are assigned to support AT services provided by an agency also need time in their official work assignment to carry out those activities. In a survey of participants in a preconference workshop at a national AT conference, the average FTE for AT teams was 2.65 (DeCoste & Bowser, 2016). Survey respondents indicated that most team members participated as only one part of their work responsibilities. Survey data indicated that only in school districts with a population of more than 50,000 students did team members typically have full-time positions on the AT team.

All educators who work with students who use AT need time to learn about, plan for, and help students use AT. Some require more time than others to learn a new skill or identify ways to incorporate a student's AT into instructional activities. Administrators can set aside time for training and meetings when needs are identified. This may involve (a) scheduling some days for study groups or professional learning communities (PLCs) to meet, (b) using a rotating substitute to free up time for teachers to attend training and practice skills learned in training, or (c) offering alternative professional development formats such as recorded webinars and video-conferencing technical assistance. It may involve coaching and mentoring on AT from AT leaders. Compensatory time and release time also can be helpful incentives.

Expertise

Whereas some AT tools such as calculators and pencil grips are simple and easily mastered, others are complex and require specific expertise. Some software, apps, and many of the high-end voice-output communication devices require specific staff training for successful operation. Educators also need to know how to integrate the use of the technology into the context of instruction. This is easier to understand in some situations than in others. Many teachers easily incorporate the use of concept mapping or outlining software into the writing process, whereas other types of AT integration may be more difficult to identify and carry out. For example, teachers often need to provide content vocabulary from social studies or science ahead of time so that it can be programmed into a voice-output communication device for a student who will not be able to be an active participant in a class discussion without it. Vocabulary may also need to be added to the word bank for a student with a learning disability who is using word prediction. This kind of advance planning step can make the difference between the success or failure of a plan to use AT.

AT leaders have a good understanding of these needs and can work with administrators to identify resources for expertise. AT leaders can also help identify specific topics such as augmentative communication or accessible educational materials that need to be addressed for particular groups of educators in the agency.

Sources to help increase expertise may come from within the school or the district, or they may even involve regional or state AT program assistance or help from private contractors. In seeking ways to increase expertise, school administrators and AT leaders can take action to determine what the status of AT knowledge is in the school, how it can be improved, and who can provide the needed expertise. In some cases, individual staff members or teams of AT leaders may take the lead in increasing everyone's expertise for specific tools. For example, in one school, the fifth-grade team decided to take the lead in learning to use voice recognition software and used their PLC time to do so. After a year of exploration, they shared what they had learned with their peers in other grade levels. The building principal committed funds to purchase the voice recognition software, and the technology coordinator, an AT leader, committed to installing it on the school network.

PLCs, such as the one described above, provide support, motivation, and onsite access to technical assistance. Administrators and AT leaders are both important to their success. Together, they can advocate for the establishment of the group, allocate time for group members to meet, monitor their progress, and report to other school leaders about the group's impact on student learning (Murphy & Lick, 2001). The AT leader can guide one or more PLC and can help identify other staff members who have the knowledge and interest to lead a study group.

Access

Much of the technology currently used in educational settings has accessibility features built into the system. Most operating systems for computers and tablets have built-in text-to-speech, which can be used by all students and can be categorized as AT for students with print disabilities. Many mobile tablets offer free apps that can support skills like communication, reading, writing, and executive function when a student needs AT. Technology connected to the Internet greatly expands educational programs' options with schedule and calendaring apps, reminders, text summarization, and a wide variety of other applications. AT leaders can help administrators make the most effective use of agency resources by ensuring that technology that is already available in the school is used when the features of that technology address the needs of students with disabilities and only purchasing new technology when free and readily available options do not meet the needs of a specific student. They can inform the administrator when new, more cost-effective, or easy-to-use AT solutions become available and make recommendations for upgrading inventory as needed.

Another aspect of management of physical resources is identifying AT that is already available in the school. Most schools have many AT tools, but not everyone may be aware of them. Students with disabilities will need to use pervasive technology such as calculators but may have to use them as AT more frequently or in a different way than their nondisabled peers. Administrators can work with AT leaders to identify common classroom tools that function as AT for a given student because of the impact of its use and ensure that they are available to all students with disabilities who need them.

In order for the wide variety of AT options to be integrated into instruction, AT leaders and administrators work together to identify a set of resources that can be provided to students and educators in their district. For example, some districts identify a set of tools that are on every computer and available to all, either free or through district licenses. When a consistent set of software applications and AT tools is available in all appropriate programs, educators and students can learn the tools more easily and be able to use those tools no matter where in the district the learning will take place.

AT might be borrowed for short-term use from a district, regional, or state lending library or local vendors. In some cases, even national vendors will allow 30- to 45-day free trial periods for AT products. In addition, vendors often will loan multiple copies of AT products for training sessions. Teachers must have access to the AT their students use so that they can learn to operate it and to develop a real sense of how to use it effectively in classroom activities. The AT leader will have explored this area and know the options available outside the district.

Resources

Identifying and obtaining needed resources takes administrative leadership. However, this is not something that the administrator must do alone. An AT committee or working group can be an effective way to identify what is needed and how it might be obtained. In many cases, district, state, or federal technology grants such as E-rate grants can include AT. Many school districts have initially used grant funds to help acquire some of the AT tools that they need to start an AT loan bank and acquire AT for individual students. Once an AT program is established, it is important to identify specific budget categories (e.g., capital outlay, consumable supplies) from which future upgrades and new AT can be purchased.

When people think of fiscal resources for AT, they tend to focus on budgeting for the purchase of AT devices. But there are other associated costs as well. For example, if an agency decides to maintain a library of AT devices that can be loaned for trial periods or long-term use by students, a cataloging and tracking system also will be needed. If sufficient funds are not allocated to equipment management, maintenance, and repair, the resources used for initial purchase may not be effectively utilized. Table 3.1 in the next section suggests some of the items that should be included when budgeting for AT use in a school district and provides two examples of district approaches.

In addition to fiscal resources, physical resources should be considered when establishing an AT program. Space must be allocated to store the devices when they are not being used. Storage units, and even costs of transporting the AT to the location where it is needed, might be included in a well-thought-out budget.

As managers, administrators also are responsible for the allocation of human resources. AT programs need to have people with the right kind of knowledge available to implement them. If AT skills are included in appropriate position descriptions, an administrator can ensure that educators with AT skills are available when IEP and IFSP teams need assistance. Administrators can work with AT leaders to allocate human resources by assigning specific people to be AT specialists, or they may identify a group of people who will provide AT technical assistance in each grade level or building. Whether a program's service delivery model uses an expert model or one of capacity building, the allocation of human resources should be driven by the program's vision of the service model.

Support

A lack of ongoing support is the final obstacle in the TEARS paradigm. Staff need ongoing consultation, coaching, and mentoring from a specialist or other knowledgeable staff member. If the agency is not able to have an AT specialist, it is often effective to have an on-site contact person in each school, who may not know everything about all of the AT tools in the district but who is willing to be an AT leader and a conduit for questions to a district identified AT resource person and a connection to more distant resources such as the Quality Indicators for Assistive Technology (QIAT) list at *www.qiat.org*. The QIAT list has more than 4,000 contributors who are generous in their willingness to share information and help others. In this role, AT leaders facilitate information sharing and problem solving. School administrators can work with AT leaders to help these on-site support persons. An administrator who values AT use, encourages AT experimentation and risk taking, and rewards teachers who seek and learn new AT skills that promote the achievement of all students can take actions such as these to create a culture of support for AT use.

Administrators Work with AT Leaders to Ensure Accountability

Although it is important to make sure a program has sufficient resources, it is also the administrator's responsibility to ensure that the program uses those resources wisely. If AT services are not cost-effective and efficient, it is possible to end up with a program that has lots of resources but is too costly to maintain. At the same time, a program that errs on the side of saving resources may do so at the expense of high-quality services. Working together, the administrator and AT leader can target areas that need development and areas for savings.

Efficiently managed AT programs have little duplication of costs and services. When AT budgeting is integrated into the agency's general budgeting and planning process, there are many opportunities to ensure efficiency. For instance, in some areas AT budgets and services have been integrated with information technology (IT) budgets. This kind of integration can result in less duplication of purchases and more efficient use of resources. Table 3.1 offers two examples of district-level budgets that address AT resources in ways that match the agency vision of service provision.

	BUDGET CATEGORY	DISTRICT A	DISTRICT B
PERSONNEL	Certified Salaries	1.0 AT specialist 0.3 occupational therapist 0.3 speech language pathologist 0.2 vision specialist	0.3 occupational therapist 0.5 speech language pathologist 0.5 teacher consultant
	Classified Salaries	1.0 AT program assistant	—
OPERATING EXPENSES: PURCHASED SERVICES	Instructional, Professional Services	6 days staff development	2 days staff development, 8 days evaluation services
	Repairs and Maintenance	Maintenance contracts for 5 devices Funding for repairs as needed	Funding for repairs as needed
	Rentals	14 months equipment rental	Use state lending library
	Printing/Copying	Manuals, handouts, operating guidelines, tech tips newsletter	Handouts
OPERATING EXPENSES: SUPPLIES AND MATERIALS	Consumable Supplies	Paper, printer cartridges, pencil grips, adapted writing tools, batteries	Paper, printer cartridges, pencil grips, adapted writing tools, batteries
	Books	Reference materials and instructional manuals	Reference materials and instructional manuals
	Nonconsumable Items ($1–$1,000)	Slant boards, adapted seating, switches, etc.	Slant boards, adapted seating, switches, etc.
	Computer Software	Various software, early childhood titles Site licenses	Various software titles; expand to middle school
OPERATING EXPENSES: CAPITAL OUTLAY	Additional Equipment (over $1,000)	Laptop computer systems, with scanners, tablet computers Augmentative communication devices	15 Chromebook computers 3 printers 1 document scanner
	Replacement Equipment (over $1,000)	Replace one augmentative communication device	Upgrade 3 computers
OPERATING EXPENSES: DUES AND FEES	Memberships and Subscriptions	AT newsletter, professional organization membership	3 state AT conference registrations
	Shipping and Device Transportation	Internal district courier services	Postage and shipping

TABLE 3.1.
Budget considerations

Another aspect of efficient management is tracking equipment. If one classroom has an expensive AT device in a storage closet, it is important to know where it is in case another child needs that device. Accurate equipment tracking can save educational agencies thousands of dollars a year. This is also a reason that state or regional equipment libraries can be so beneficial. Another strategy is to participate in bulk purchase or volume licensing agreements whenever possible. Once the volume license is purchased, dissemination of information about the license can ensure cost-effective use.

Ensuring that AT evaluations are completed in-house as often as possible, either by the IEP team or with the help of a school district AT team, is also a cost-effective strategy. Relying on outside evaluators for most AT evaluations is expensive and may not yield the desired results if the assessor does not understand the student's environment. Additionally, research found that the further removed the AT evaluators are from the student's customary environment, the more complex and expensive the recommended AT may be (Behrmann & Schepis, 1994).

Administrators Work with AT Leaders to Ensure Equity of Access

Administrators have the unique ability to ensure equity of access to AT tools across the programs they supervise. Building administrators can ensure that all teachers in their building have access to AT tools for their own learning and for use with students. District-level administrators can ensure this same level of access throughout the district. Service providers need access to both hardware and software to try out, learn to operate, and use for trials with students prior to purchase (McInerney, Osher, & Kane, 1997). Large school districts may be able to provide this for themselves, but smaller school districts will need to collaborate with other districts or seek assistance from an education service agency, their state educational agency, or their state Tech Act program. The Florida Assistive Technology Educational Network, the Georgia Project for Assistive Technology, the Oregon Technology Access Program, and many other successful state AT projects operate AT lending libraries that are open to all school districts in their states.

Administrators also can ensure equity of access to training by bringing training into their building or district, taking advantage of online training, and requiring staff to come back and train others when they have attended conferences or workshops. Successful administrators redirect resources as needed to build competence and support high standards (Brewer, 2001). Ensuring that AT use is a part of routine transition is an example. It is costly and shortsighted to determine the AT need, provide it, train the staff, train the student, have that student experience success, and then move on to the next grade only to find that the technology is not available, the teacher doesn't know how to use it, or the teacher doesn't understand the need for it. Only an administrator can ensure the money and effort that are expended in the first setting are not wasted in the next one.

Management: Getting Started

Management is the part of administration that makes it possible to improve programs and lead a program toward attainment of a commonly held vision. Administrators and AT leaders can work together to ensure that management tasks get done, that guidelines are developed and implemented, and that any problems are recognized early and addressed effectively.

Actions for Administrators

- Develop (or review) processes and operating guidelines for AT services.

- Allocate physical, personnel, time, and monetary resources

- Ensure accountability for AT services by working with the AT leader to use cost-effective acquisition strategies.

- Identify opportunities that you typically have where advocating for AT use might be appropriate and effective.

Actions for AT Leaders

- Establish a system for tracking, distribution, and management of equipment.

- Research and organize volume licensing and bulk purchases.

- Gather and maintain data about devices used by students throughout the district.

- Maintain a list of AT devices needed by the district based on current and future student needs.

CHAPTER 4

Supervision for AT Services

Use this chapter to develop coordinated systems of supervision and professional development to ensure that educators have the skills and the feedback they need in order to provide effective AT services for students with disabilities.

- ✔ Assess staff AT knowledge, skills, performance, and training needs.

- ✔ Recruit individuals with AT skills.

- ✔ Ensure that all staff, including general education teachers, have the necessary understanding of AT to fulfill their role in supporting the use of AT by students with disabilities in their classes.

- ✔ Demonstrate interest and support for making AT available and usable by students as part of staff evaluation and supervision.

- ✔ Ensure that all staff members who serve a child with a disability implement the IEP, including any use of AT, in a legal and ethical manner.

- ✔ Foster a school environment that has a low level of conflict and assist in conflict resolution including conflict around AT.

- ✔ Support teams as they work to make AT available to students with disabilities by providing structure and clear expectations.

As supervisors of many different employees who work with students with disabilities and support those students in the use of AT devices, administrators have a unique opportunity to ensure that AT is on the radar screen for everyone. Although evaluating staff within mandated timelines is important, supervision involves much more. AT knowledge can be part of both the hiring and ongoing training of staff. Only administrators have the assigned responsibility to recruit staff members who are qualified to provide AT services, ensure that the AT services provided are legal and ethical, and help create a positive learning environment that supports and expects functional and effective AT use as part of a high-quality education for students with disabilities.

Supervision duties provide administrators with a significant opportunity to impact the quality of AT services in the programs they administer. In their role as supervisors, administrators can

- recruit individuals with knowledge about technology, including AT;

- hire highly qualified staff whose skills include experience with all types of technology, including AT, where possible;

- include a focus on the staff member's work with students who use AT as part of staff observations;

- include criteria about the responsibility to understand AT and support its use by students on staff evaluation forms;

- facilitate individual staff members to work together as teams to support students using AT;

- encourage collaboration and cooperation among all staff in supporting students who use AT; and

- foster a positive and productive climate for the use of AT and learning.

AT leaders can assist administrators in these activities by identifying appropriate resources and helping to develop specific job descriptions, interview questions, and staff performance monitoring procedures.

Staff Knowledge and Skills

Not every person on a student's IEP team needs to know everything about the AT that student uses. A resource room teacher may need different information than the information that an educational assistant or a general education teacher does. None would require the same level of expertise as the person identified as an AT leader. Even though not everyone needs the same level of AT expertise, every educator who works with a child who uses AT must have some basic knowledge. It is important that educators be sufficiently knowledgeable to carry out their assigned roles in making AT an effective, well-integrated part of a child's overall educational program.

Here is what everyone on the student-services team should know:

- the definition of AT devices and services according to IDEA,

- the school district's responsibility to provide AT,

- factors that indicate that a student might need AT,

- actions for effective participation in AT consideration during the IEP meeting,

- individuals to contact within the building or district to find out more about AT,

- the agency's process to make a referral for AT when needed, and

- strategies to determine whether the AT, when provided, is making a difference.

Some of the items in this list are general information, whereas others relate to district processes (e.g., AT consideration, making a referral). To facilitate the completion of these steps, staff members must have access to all the information. The single most helpful action that administrators can take is to develop, disseminate, and implement effective AT procedures. This is a good example of how all aspects of an administrator's job come together.

Staff also need essential information about specific students in their classroom, including: (a) the goals, objectives, and specific services listed in each student's IEP, (b) background information that explains the reason for the AT tools, (c) directions for operating the specific AT being provided, and (d) general ideas about how to support the student's use of the AT. An AT leader, in collaboration with an administrator, can support staff by ensuring that they have the information they need to help their students using AT to be more active and successful participants in their educational programs.

Is AT Making a Difference?

One of the most important aspects of effective AT services is determining whether the AT is making a difference. An AT leader can be a valuable resource to help educators identify the information that will be needed to make that determination and to set up the process to gather and analyze information. AT evaluation of effectiveness strategies might include review of the following:

- work samples completed with and without the AT, evaluated with rubrics to pinpoint patterns of performance;

- results of formative assessments such as chapter tests;

- scores on formal tests;

- observed changes in engagement with and without the AT; and

- student self-report of preferences for using (or not using) the AT, any changes in time or effort required to complete work, and how the AT helps.

When analyzed periodically according to a previously determined schedule, this information can help guide the effective use of AT and highlight additional areas of need.

For example, a fifth-grade teacher who is providing universally designed learning opportunities determined that one of her students with an identified learning disability in the area of writing produced significantly improved answers to the questions at the end of the chapter in both science and social studies when using speech-to-text to "write" his responses. Before an IEP meeting, she compared his responses when required to use handwriting or keyboarding to his responses using speech-to-text. The quality and quantity were both much better. The student was able to demonstrate a deeper understanding of the material covered in the chapters when he used speech-to-text. That difference made her realize that he benefited significantly from the use of speech-to-text as an assistive feature when being asked to write assignments. She shared that data in his IEP meeting, and because of it, during AT consideration, the IEP team determined that he needed AT in the form of speech-to-text for all longer writing assignments and included it in his IEP.

Often the tool that is an assistive technology tool for a specific student is a routinely available tool or a feature for all students but one that makes a significant difference in the performance of an individual with a disability. When this is true, the role of the classroom teacher is to recognize when the student needs the technology as AT, and the responsibility of the IEP team during AT consideration is to look for those instances and document them in the IEP so that the student doesn't lose access to a valuable tool that can help him be successful. Writing AT into the IEP is the only way to ensure that the technology feature will be provided for the student in future classroom placements.

SETTING THE TONE　**David Fortunato, Teacher, Chesapeake High School, Baltimore, MD**

"The principal and administration set the tone for the building. They have the ability to implement the use of AT within the academic environment. Special education can do only so much. But within the general education areas, administrators have the ability to force the issue. They can open doors where the nonadministrator cannot. I see the value of AT, and I told our county AT specialist to send any AT that needs to be tested to our high school. We will find a way to use it.

"We are lucky at Chesapeake High School to have a principal who is flexible in allowing his staff to implement services that will raise the academic potential of all students. He also sees the value of AT. A couple of months ago, I attended a meeting where we were discussing the implementation of the Kurzweil Reading Program. Chesapeake High School was far ahead of the other schools in using the software. If it were not for the support of our principal and the administrative team, I believe that this would have been a very difficult sell. I am a social studies teacher and I use the Kurzweil Program with students on an almost daily basis."

Building a Team

Administrators can make an enormous difference in the provision of AT devices and services if they understand how each position fits into the larger picture of AT use. It can be useful to spend some time thinking about the performance requirements of each position as it applies to AT. The skills related to AT needed by people in each position may not relate directly to the level of overall responsibility for the child's instruction (see Table 4.1). For example, in some situations educational assistants need to know more about the technical operation of an AT device than the special education teacher does. That is because they may be more directly involved in the day-to-day operation of the device. A special education teacher, on the other hand, should know how the use of that AT relates to the student's IEP goals and needs to be able to determine the most practical times in the day to implement its use.

		TABLE 4.1. AT information needed according to role
General education teacher	Student's curriculum, goals, and objectives and how the AT will be used to meet them How student will use AT for academics and/or in functional life skills New AT skills the student is working on Who to contact to get help with the AT	
Instructional assistant	Setup, operation, and troubleshooting of specific hardware or software used by students in the classroom Specific activities and times when the student uses the AT Data collection strategies How to get help with the AT	
Special education teacher	Long-term vision of AT use Setup, operation, and application of AT in the classroom How to modify the student's AT program based on data Student's curriculum, goals, and objectives, and how AT will be used to achieve them	
Speech and language pathologist	Student's current level of language function Student's curriculum, goals, and objectives, and how AT will be used to develop or demonstrate language skills Setup and operation of augmentative communication devices Speech and language assessment and data collection strategies Speech and language goal, and activity modification strategies based on data	
Occupational therapist	Student's motor function and how it relates to AT use Adaptation of the environment to ensure access Adaptation and modification of the AT when it is needed Seating and positioning for optimal AT use	
AT specialist	Student's curriculum, goals, and objectives, and how AT will be used to achieve them Setup, operation, and application of a wide range of AT Troubleshooting strategies for AT Resources for AT repair and maintenance AT assessment, implementation, and data collection strategies AT program modification strategies based on effectiveness data	
Instructional technology specialist	How AT interfaces with existing computer systems How AT interfaces with local area networks How AT interfaces with wide area networks Selection of software and hardware for general use that includes features that can meet the needs of children with disabilities (e.g., text-to-speech, screen enlargement) Advanced hardware and software troubleshooting skills that can be applied to AT	

AT service delivery takes a team to make it work well. Just as each discipline has something to contribute to the development of a student's overall educational program, when it includes AT, no one individual has all the information needed. One team member may have expertise in seating, positioning, and device mounting; another brings knowledge of critical aspects of language development; and yet another understands the curricular requirements and most relevant daily opportunities for use of the AT. So the team that serves the individual child must all be involved in the planning and delivery of support to that child.

If there is an AT team, that team will also need support and supervision. The tasks of the AT team generally center on the selection, acquisition, and use of AT and the support of other teams and individuals who are serving individual students. However, there is a significant difference in specific tasks and actions, based on whether the AT team's goal is to provide direct services to students or to develop the capacity of other school district staff. Based on the vision of what they want to accomplish, the team can work with the AT leader and administrator to plan the specific tasks they will undertake to achieve that vision. The norms of team operation develop quickly during the first few meetings, either intentionally or unintentionally. Teams may end up with significant problems if they do not spend at least part of their time talking about and planning for their operating procedures. Defining and then rotating roles such as facilitator, following clear processes, and using consensus in reaching decisions are important aspects that require the team's attention.

Not every AT team member needs to know the same thing. Rather, the team members should strive to augment each other's work as they plan for their own skill development. Administrators can encourage teams to consider what each member brings to the team and what specific new skills are needed to enhance team function and the student's AT program. AT leaders can help teams to identify the new information and skills they need to enhance their performance with AT, and administrators can support the development of those skills through arranging for individual professional development opportunities and requiring that individuals share what they learned during professional development with other team members. For example, an administrator can create an application form to be used when professionals request attendance at professional development opportunities outside the district. The application might require that the individual identify the goals for professional learning, but also think about how that information will be shared with other staff members after returning to the district.

Recently Google spent two years studying effective teams (Duhigg, 2016). The most successful ones shared five traits. Surprisingly, the most successful teams did not have specific ways of operating in common. Instead, they had in common group norms that govern how they function as a team. The study outlined five key characteristics of effective teams:

Psychological safety: Feeling safe to take risks, voice their opinions, and ask judgment-free questions are important to team members.

Dependability: Knowing that fellow team members get things done on time and meet expectations is also important.

Structure and clarity: High-performing teams have clear goals, and well-defined roles within the group.

Meaning: Work that has personal significance to each member results in high performance.

Impact: Believing their work is purposeful and is having a positive impact for the greater good is another critical aspect.

Google found that teams with these characteristics had employees who were less likely to leave, more likely to harness the power of diversity, and ultimately more successful.

When reviewing team performance, administrators and AT leaders might ask themselves questions like the following based on DeCoste, Reed, and Kaplan (2005) and Heathfield (2017) as they work to build effective teams that address students' use of AT devices and services:

- **Clear expectations:** Do team members, administrators, and other staff members hold shared expectations for what should be accomplished when AT is considered? How are those expectations communicated?

- **Context:** Do team members understand and appreciate why they are working as a team rather than as individuals? Do team members expect their AT skills to grow and develop as a result of working on the team? Is the team's role and purpose for AT understood by others in the school?

- **Competence:** Do team members feel that the appropriate people are participating? Do they feel they each have the AT skill, knowledge, and capability needed to accomplish their purpose? If not, do they feel they have access to resources and training?

- **Charter:** Has the school administration clearly identified teams' authority to make AT recommendations, implement plans, and garner cooperation from others?

- **Control:** Does the team have sufficient support and latitude so that team members feel they can accomplish needed AT tasks? At the same time, do team members clearly understand their boundaries?

- **Collaboration:** Does the team understand and use specific AT group processes, especially for decision making? Do team members work together effectively? Has the team established group norms for things like conflict resolution and consensus reaching?

- **Communication:** Do team members communicate clearly and honestly with each other in a timely fashion? Are important issues discussed? Are diverse opinions welcomed and invited?

- **Consequences:** Do team members feel responsible and accountable for team achievements? Are AT successes viewed and celebrated as team accomplishments rather than individual accomplishments?

Administrators must have a different knowledge base than the educators they supervise and support. Rather than focusing on the needs of individual students, administrators and AT leaders must focus on big-picture questions, including these:

- What AT is being used by the full range of students in the building or program?

- In what situations might each student be expected to use his AT?

- How should educators determine whether AT is being used effectively in their classrooms?

- In general, what skills will the staff members serving students who use AT need to know

- Who in the district can provide training when educators need to learn new skills?

- Who in the district can troubleshoot any problems that occur with the AT?

Big-picture information is essential for administrators in their role as supervisors. In Principal Mary's case (sidebar), she found an unacceptable situation and used her supervisory responsibilities to spotlight a problem situation and help to change it. AT leaders are the individuals most likely to know which students are using AT and the goals for that AT usage. An AT leader can also be a source of information and guidance about how the use of the AT might be expected to change the student's performance.

It can be very effective for AT leaders to regularly provide an AT information sheet to the building principal or other administrator whose job it is to evaluate teachers. This sheet can list the students who have AT in their IEP, what task that AT supports, and what changes might be expected. AT leaders are also aware of the specific knowledge and skills needed by teachers to support the use of their students' AT devices and the best source of training for that knowledge and skill.

MARY'S STORY: THE ASSIGNED LEADER

When Mary began her new position as principal, she knew that she wanted to let all the staff know that she valued good instruction and engaged learners. To that end, she made it a point to drop into each classroom for just a few minutes each week. She varied the time and stayed just a few minutes. She knew she could manage this only for a few weeks, but she wanted to set the tone early in the school year.

As part of this process, she visited the special education classrooms. The Learning Resource Center seemed to be going well, there was a buzz of learning activity, and teachers and paraprofessionals were engaged in instructing or supporting the students in various ways. When she entered the classroom for students with severe physical and multiple disabilities, the students looked happy but they didn't appear engaged in any educational tasks. She greeted several of the students. Six of them were apparently not able to speak, but they smiled and in some cases made a non-intelligible sound.

When Mary asked the teacher about communicating with these students, the teacher's response was vague and not at all informative. Mary decided she needed more information. She called the special education director to ask for help. She learned that she was responsible for evaluating the special education teachers in her building and that there was an AT specialist in the district who had assessed each of these students and helped to acquire voice output communication devices for them.

Mary met with the AT specialist and the special education teacher. Together, they reviewed the students' IEPs. The IEP for each of the students included specific goals for using their voice output communication devices. They also indicated that the speech and language pathologist (SLP) provided services to those students weekly.

Mary made it a point to stop by the classroom when the SLP was there. She noted that the SLP set up the devices, updated vocabulary, and set up opportunities for the students to practice using their devices. Mary invited the special education director, AT specialist, SLP, and teacher to a meeting where she expressed her concerns that the students were not getting a chance to communicate and that the IEPs were not being implemented. Together, they developed a plan to remediate problems they had identified. Later, Mary asked the special education teacher to work with her to develop one professional development goal regarding the use of AT. This goal would be included as a part of the teacher's evaluation in the following year. As an informed administrator, Mary had the ability to change the situation. Her supervision activities helped mitigate a significant problem.

Determining Professional Development Needs

There is a need for professional development about AT. Studies repeatedly show that both special education and general education teachers receive very little training about AT in their teacher preparation programs. Judge and Simms (2009) found that only one-third of undergraduate special education programs require an AT course and that less than one-quarter of the master's programs required one AT course.

Because the field of AT also changes rapidly, professional development is needed to help educators stay abreast of new tools and strategies. In addition, studies have found that teachers who receive 40 or more hours of AT training report that it is essential to students' daily activities. Teachers who have not received AT training report that it is not important, that they are not confident in identifying and using AT with students, and that they are more reluctant to use it (Alnahdi, 2014; Ashton, Lee, & Vega, 2005; Johnstone, Thurlow, Altman, Timmons, & Kato, 2009). A program of professional development in the area of AT is an important district-wide concern. Only administrators can make time available for AT training and encourage teachers to participate. AT leaders can help administrators identify specific topics and training resources, as well as target key groups most in need of training.

Figure 4.1 shows a sample general needs assessment that can be used to look more closely at the specific AT skills of staff members. Once educators have a picture of the kinds of AT skills they should have, administrators can help them develop those skills by including AT in school improvement goals, individual professional development plans, and annual performance goals. AT leaders can help them by sharing useful resources, regularly sending out tips and suggestions, and providing specific training. A general education teacher in a second-grade classroom might have a goal of learning how to use one or two specific pieces of software. A resource room teacher's goal might include learning to use a particular AT assessment framework. A related service provider might focus on improving AT training skills. Each staff member's professional development plan that includes AT can be tailored to the particular job responsibilities and unique needs of the individual.

FIGURE 4.1.
AT Training Needs Assessment

WRITE NUMBERS 1 THROUGH 5 BY YOUR FIVE MOST CRITICAL TRAINING NEEDS, IN ORDER OF IMPORTANCE.	
	Learn more about the range of AT for (Please check the ones of most interest): ___ Writing ___ Reading ___ Communication ___ Studying/Organizing information ___ Math ___ Vision ___ Hearing ___ Other:_____
	Effectively consider the need for AT in IEP meetings.
	Work as part of a team to complete an evaluation of a child to determine if she/he could benefit from AT, including using informal assessment techniques (e.g., environmental inventory, interview, and observation).
	Access appropriate funding sources for AT, including write/compile necessary documentation to support funding from third parties.
	Write IEP/IFSP goals/objectives as needed to describe the use of AT.
	Determine for an individual student when the best intervention is to teach a new skill, teach a compensatory skill, use AT, or use a personal assistant.
	Determine appropriate use of AT as an accommodation or modification in order to participate in standardized testing, including district and state assessments.
	Understand the use and operation of a specific AT or AAC devices: _____ _____

AT leaders can support administrators by working with staff to understand student needs, abilities, educational goals, and environmental factors that relate to the selection and delivery of AT devices and services. They can then identify training needs, and provide training, technical assistance, and coaching to address student, staff, and family needs. Research shows that coaching is a critical factor in implementing information learned in training (Turner & McCarthy, 2015).

Coaching as a support strategy has been shown to account for large gains among educators in knowledge about new skills, in the ability to demonstrate skills, and most important, in their ability to effectively apply skills in the classroom with students (Joyce & Showers, 2002; Truesdale, 2003). Effective coaching can help educators apply new practices in classroom environments, establish a safe environment for improvement, develop leadership skills, and support the work of colleagues (Neufeld & Roper, 2003).

Recruiting Knowledgeable Staff

An important aspect of staff supervision is recruitment of new educational staff members. When administrators have examined each position with a focus on the AT requirements of that position, they are better able to ask interview questions about the prospective employee's knowledge of both instructional and assistive technologies. This is particularly useful when filling positions that require AT skills. It also is extremely helpful in building a staff where members consider AT to be an important component in the full range of tools and strategies they use to help children with disabilities in all aspects of education. In addition, it serves as an indicator to applicants that knowledge and skill in AT are valuable and desirable.

Teacher job descriptions typically include responsibilities related to technology. For example, an elementary teacher job description might include these responsibilities:

- provide a variety of learning materials and resources for use in educational activities,

- identify and select different instructional resources and methods to meet students' varying needs,

- instruct and monitor students in the use of learning materials and equipment, and

- use relevant technology to support instruction.

The management and use of AT fits well into those typical requirements and can be made more explicit either in the job description by adding the words "including AT" to one or more of the requirements or by asking specific questions in job interviews that address a teacher's willingness and ability to provide access to a student's AT in daily activities, plan for and include its use in daily lesson plans, and monitor the student's skill development in using it to complete tasks and make progress in the curriculum.

General technology competencies can also be helpful as a general guide to the nature of AT competencies that are needed. A good resource is the International Society for Technology in Education (ISTE). ISTE developed National Education Technology Standards (NETS) for students, teachers, and administrators at *www.iste.org*. Within the Standards for Teachers, 5a states, "Use technology to create, adapt and personalize learning experiences that foster independent learning and accommodate learner differences and needs." The phrase "learner differences and needs" shows that AT is regarded as a way to accommodate those needs.

For special educators, related service providers, and AT staff, more specific competencies might be included in position descriptions or criteria for staff evaluations. For example:

- match needs of students with disabilities to appropriate features of AT devices (e.g., hardware, software, or apps) to meet educational needs;

- monitor outcomes of AT use by students and reevaluate, change, or adjust the AT as needed; and

- work with team members to identify and implement AT to help individual students to meet the demands of the curriculum and specific tasks.

Monitoring Staff Performance in Relation to AT

There are specific observations that can be helpful to administrators in determining whether staff members are fulfilling their roles in the provision of AT devices and services.

During the IEP meeting, the administrator can listen for

- AT to be discussed during the special factors discussion about the need for AT, and that it is not dismissed out of hand because IEP team members do not understand the law or the importance of AT;

- during that discussion, more than one AT tool is explored because team members are familiar with a variety of AT;

- a clear relationship between the AT and the goals it can help the student to achieve;

- documentation of the AT in a logical way in the IEP; and

- a well-laid-out plan for any needed trials of new AT before long-term use.

During classroom walk-throughs or observations, an administrator can look for these signs that AT services are being provided:

- students who have AT in their IEP have it available to them in good working order at appropriate times;

- AT is used for necessary tasks so that the student using it is actively engaged in learning activities;

- during the course of the year, students who use AT are gaining skills in its operation or use and can demonstrate them; and

- personnel in the student's environments have the knowledge they need to keep the AT operational (set it up, troubleshoot and solve simple problems, and know who to contact for bigger problems).

During informal discussions, an administrator can listen for

- positive comments or appropriate questions about the AT from staff;

- knowledgeable discussion of the ways in which AT is helping students meet goals and objectives, complete tasks, and make progress in the curriculum; and

- awareness of the need to plan for effective transition to the next grade or school so that the AT will continue to be used.

Conversely, administrators can note red flags related to AT. These include

- AT consideration in the IEP meeting is typically cursory, with little or no discussion;

- AT is rarely mentioned when brainstorming about how student progress can be increased;

- teachers do not seem to know that AT is included in a student's IEP, or how it is being implemented;

- negative conversations about AT or AT service providers take place; and

- the AT specialist seems to be working in isolation with little or no involvement of teachers.

In both formal and informal interactions, administrators can make sure that teachers are acknowledged for effective use of AT in their classrooms. Administrators can provide specific feedback about what was noticed and what seems to be going well. Simply paying attention to and mentioning AT can be powerful motivation for teachers to think about and effectively support AT use by their students.

Staff Evaluation

When administrators include AT in their staff evaluations, educators see it as important. Inclusion of AT questions in the staff evaluation interview, when appropriate, can help set an expectation within the entire school that educators will be as knowledgeable about their AT responsibilities as they are about reading, math, motor skills, or behavior management. The fourth-grade teacher who has a student who uses a voice output device might be asked how he integrates that student's device into daily instruction. The special education teacher who supports students with disabilities in an inclusive setting might be asked what resources she has provided and what specific steps she has taken to support the fourth-grade teacher's use of AT and help her identify how to incorporate the AT as effortlessly as possible. Just asking questions can make a difference.

Professional Development about AT

Professional development (or training) is a primary component of providing quality supervision in education. Professional development is most effective when it is related to overall school goals and based on identified needs. As Table 4.1 demonstrates, each service provider has a different role in the provision of AT services. Therefore, their training needs will vary. In addition, each individual will bring different knowledge, skills, and interests to each position. The most effective staff development content: (a) is planned in response to assessed needs, (b) is presented in a variety of modes, and (c) matches the knowledge level of the participants. Joyce and Showers (2002) also found that content that is concrete and aimed at developing specific, usable skills is more effective than simply introducing new concepts. Although important, learning that AT can make a difference for students is not enough. Teachers also must learn how and why to select and use specific tools to address specific student needs.

A variety of ways are available to provide effective professional development on AT. They include

- written materials, manuals, and textbooks;

- online resources;

- overview and introductory workshops;

- attendance at local, state, and national AT conferences;

- specific training on AT consideration during the IEP, assessing students' need for AT, and implementation of AT use in the classroom;

- open labs and demonstrations conducted by AT staff;

- tutorials and tip sheets;

- training on specific devices or software; and

- participation in a study group or learning community.

We have long known that research on the effectiveness of training shows it must include multiple sessions, spread over time, that take place in the school environment and must be presented by trainers who have credibility with the participants (Butler, 1992). In addition to organized training sessions, effective staff development may include individuals or small groups seeking information and working independently and to apply it in their context.

For example, the AT Internet Modules at *www.atinternetmodules.org* are excellent resources and include multiple modules on AT services. There is a module on AT Consideration in the IEP Process. It includes a short video simulation of a student's IEP team considering his need for AT. There is an introductory module on AT Evaluation and a complete training program devoted to the Wisconsin Assistive Technology Initiative (WATI) process for AT assessment. Each one is focused on AT tools for a specific area of concern, including writing, communication, mobility, computer access, and many more.

Other useful online resources include the following:

For Administrators and AT Leaders

The sample operating guidelines at *www.douglasesd.k12.or.us/otap/publications* are designed to be used as templates by education agencies wishing to develop AT programs that provide consistent, effective, and legal AT services. Section 1 includes guidance for teams that can be included in district handbooks or procedure manuals. Section 2 includes sample forms that may be used to implement the model.

The Quality Indicators for Assistive Technology website (*www.qiat.org*) contains a wealth of information. Two of the most important items are the Quality Indicators themselves and the QIAT Self-Evaluation Matrix. These two tools provide an excellent picture of what AT services should be—regardless of size, location, or wealth of a school district. The self-evaluation matrix is a valuable tool for getting a sense of what a specific district may need to focus on to improve its services.

Neighborhood Legal Services, Inc., has a series of booklets on legal issues related to AT: *www.nls.org/Disability/NationalAssistiveTechnologyProject*.

For Staff

The Georgia Project for Assistive Technology (*www.gpat.org*) has many excellent resources on its website, including an AT Resource Guide that provides a continuum of solutions from standard tools to AT. It also includes potential modifications and accommodations for a variety of tasks. Under Considering Assistive Technology for Students with Disabilities, choose Assistive Technology Resource Guide.

The High Incidence Accessible Technology (HIAT) website from Montgomery County (MD) Public Schools (*www.montgomeryschoolsmd.org/departments/hiat-tech/*) is a wealth of information for educators. Its goal is to support teachers who are using technology to support all students. The site has excellent resources, including many technology tip sheets and videos.

The Texas Assistive Technology Network has excellent training modules (*www.texasat.net/training-modules/training-modules-home*), including Considering AT in the IEP Process.

The Wisconsin Assistive Technology Initiative website (*www.wati.org*) provides free copies of the WATI AT Assessment forms that can be downloaded as well as a wealth of information on AT devices and AT assessments. The 2017 WATI Assessment forms can be downloaded by clicking on the link at the bottom of the first page.

AbleData (*www.abledata.com*) is a federally sponsored site that contains information on thousands of AT products.

Ability Hub (*http://abilityhub.com/*) offers information about adaptive equipment and alternative ways to access a computer. It is a searchable site that can reduce the time it takes to locate a potential tool.

For Parents

Understood (*www.understood.org/en/school-learning/assistive-technology*) is designed by and for parents. It provides excellent, accurate, easy-to-understand information about a variety of topics, including AT.

The Education Tech Points (*www.educationtechpoints.org*) website includes a free manual to download. *Hey! Can I Try That?* is designed to be used with teens and preteens to help them think about tasks that are difficult and how AT could help them. Its purpose is to promote self-determination.

Coaching

No matter what the structure, high-quality professional development is grounded in inquiry, collaborative, sustained, ongoing, and intensive (Joyce & Showers, 2002). Effective professional development for educators is connected to their work with students, engages them in concrete tasks, and must be connected to other aspects of school change (Neufeld & Roper, 2003). As part of the process to develop or improve an AT program, this means it is important to shift the focus from stand-alone sessions about the operation of devices and/or software to a more comprehensive approach to professional development that includes specific imple-mentation strategies and ongoing support.

Studies have also shown that there is a high level of anxiety about learning to use technology and that the anxiety detracts from the participants' ability to learn and may even create a resistance to learning (Sam, Othman, & Nordin, 2005). New learning that is outside the experience of the trainee or new learning that requires a more complex repertoire of skills is more difficult for trainees and demands greater planning and precision from the trainers (Joyce & Showers, 2002).

Unfortunately, training offered as the only type of intervention, no matter how well done, does not result in effective implementation. Training alone, as a method of change, has repeatedly been shown to be ineffective in human services, edu-cation, health, business, and manufacturing (Fixsen, Naoom, Blasé, Friedman, & Wallace, 2005). In addition, there is good evidence that successful implementation of any new strategy requires a longer-term, multilevel approach. In a review of the literature of the kinds of supports that are effective in making educational change, Joyce and Showers (2002) found that even when well-designed training is paired with demonstration and opportunities to practice during professional development sessions, educators are generally able to retain and implement only 20% of the con-tent provided. During the implementation phase of the AT program development process, AT leaders and other persons providing support must understand what knowledge and skill trainees have and what additional skills are needed. Coaching is the primary support strategy that increases the trainee's ability to retain and apply new information to almost 90% of the content provided (Joyce & Showers, 2002).

Coaching makes such a powerful difference because an effective AT coach does not tell people what to do but asks them to examine their own thinking behind what they're currently doing in order to act more consistently toward accomplishing their goals. In establishing a coaching relationship, the coach emphasizes the opportunity to reflect on and analyze the situation through the use of respectful questions, active listening, and the provision of clear and responsive feedback. The focus of a coaching relationship is on the capacity of the person who receives the support rather than the content to be applied. The role of a coach is not so much to be an expert or partner in the endeavor as it is to be a mediator of thinking and a catalyst for change. Coaching as a support strategy accounts for large gains among educators in knowledge about the new skills, in the ability to demonstrate skills, and most important, in their ability to effectively apply skills in the classroom with students (Joyce & Showers, 2002; Truesdale, 2003). Effective coaching can help trainees apply new practices in classroom environments, establish a safe environment for improvement, develop leadership skills, and support the work of colleagues (Neufeld & Roper, 2003).

Providing Legal and Ethical Services

It can sometimes be challenging to provide legal and ethical services that comply with all requirements of the various laws governing education. IDEA includes a variety of procedural guidelines for services provided to children with disabilities. Each of these guidelines applies to AT devices and services in the same way that it applies to specially designed instruction and related services. School administrators can help the people they supervise to understand and comply with these requirements. There are timelines for assessment and provision of services, as well as documentation and privacy requirements. Each of these requirements comes into play when AT devices and services are provided.

Monitoring staff's success in providing all services listed in students' IEPs, including AT, is an important aspect of the administrator's role. Failure to implement the IEP is one of the most common complaints about students' special education programs (Miller, 2003). The nature of the difficulty with AT is that, to be effective, it must be used in meaningful tasks during customary activities. This requires that the classroom teacher and instructional assistant, if one is present, be sufficiently skilled to help a student use AT on a daily basis. AT specialists, occupational therapists, or speech/language pathologists who are itinerant service providers cannot do this. They can provide needed training, make suggestions, and help problem solve and troubleshoot, but they cannot make available the daily opportunities for meaningful use. At the same time, they are not supervisors and have not been assigned a responsibility to monitor teacher performance. Related service providers and teachers are essentially equals. Only an administrator can require the specific actions necessary to ensure the implementation of the IEP. AT leaders can alert school administrators to situations where students are not making adequate progress despite efforts to implement an AT plan, but they are not usually empowered to take any formal action with staff to remedy the situation.

Classroom teachers are also the only people who can fully integrate the use of AT with instructional strategies. For example, while students frequently struggle with multiple aspects of a task such as writing, technology alone rarely addresses all of the students' writing needs (Fennema-Jansen, 2001). Rather, students need instruction in specific writing skills combined with AT use to assist them with specific steps of the writing task.

Ensuring continuity from year to year is another important contribution of the administrator. If a teacher is new, hasn't read the IEP, or is not very technology savvy, AT may not be used even though a student is skilled in using it and accustomed to having it available. Only administrators can ensure that student time, teacher time, and tax dollars are not wasted because AT in which the district has already invested time and money is not used.

Administrators can set the example of embracing AT as a valued tool for students. They can do this through formal staff evaluations and informal exchanges throughout the school year. They can set examples in discussions with parents as well as staff. Whether or not they are aware of it, administrators set the tone for how AT is valued by staff. Negative comments, lack of attention to student growth in relation to AT, and focus on costs can all lead staff to believe that AT is not desired, valued, or important. The attitudes and actions a school administrator models will be reflected in the educators she supervises.

Resources for Conflict Resolution

It's no different to have conflict about what happened to the football team last week than it is to have conflict about AT. Parents disagree. Staff members disagree. An effective administrator has a system for approaching conflict that applies to any situation that may arise.

Teams that are considering AT should know what to do when conflict arises. Administrators can help teams identify and practice strategies for resolving conflict. They also can set guidelines regarding who should be notified when conflict arises and when that notification should occur. When disagreements go beyond the difference of opinion, supervisors can identify resources within the agency or even outside of it that will help the team come to a resolution.

AT leaders can help by noting disagreements, providing resources and information to colleagues who are in disagreement, and sharing relevant information with the administrator in a timely fashion.

An administrator can use a variety of techniques to work out disagreements about AT devices and services, including the following:

Data-based assessment and trial periods—One excellent way to resolve conflict is to identify the specific role that AT is to play in a particular student's life. Teams then collect initial data, identify the questions they want to answer, collect more data, and then review that data. In many cases, clearly identifying the questions, by itself, helps to resolve the conflict. When team members are not all working to answer the same questions, there is greater likelihood of conflict (Reed, Bowser, & Korsten, 2002).

Adding team members with expertise—Sometimes team members may disagree because they do not have enough information about the student, the technology they are considering, or the ways that the technology can be used. Adding a person to the team who has experience with the AT solution, or one who knows the child's curriculum, or one who understands the specifics of the child's disability can provide the needed information. In some cases, the person may be an AT specialist, but in others it may be a person who is knowledgeable about the student's motor, cognitive, or language functioning.

Independent educational evaluation—Independent educational evaluations (IEEs) are included in IDEA as a required option for parents when they disagree with a team decision. Each education agency is required to maintain a list of qualifications for an independent educational evaluator and a list of local evaluators who meet those qualifications. When an IEE is requested regarding AT, administrators can access that list to help to find someone who is qualified to complete the IEE at the district's expense.

While administrators may be able to help resolve conflict when it arises, the more proactive approach is to facilitate and support collaboration in environments where AT is used (McGivern & McKevitt, 2002). Administrators as supervisors can work with AT leaders to ensure that all staff members have the knowledge and skills they need to provide AT services that are effective, ethical, legal, and cost efficient.

Supervision: Getting Started

Supervision activities bring the administrator into direct contact with all of the staff members who are supporting students as they use their assistive technology. This offers administrators many opportunities to encourage and promote the use of AT.

Actions for Administrators

- Identify the AT knowledge needed by each staff member in order to fulfill his or her responsibilities to educate children with disabilities.

- Identify the AT leader who can help you better understand AT and your staff needs related to it.

- Using the results of your self-assessment, support teams as they work to make AT available to students with disabilities by providing structure and clear expectations.

- Review hiring practices to determine where AT fits into job announcements, job descriptions, application forms, and interview questions.

- Review forms used during staff evaluations to determine where AT is appropriately addressed.

- Determine how existing conflict management practices can be applied to AT issues.

Actions for AT Leaders

- Help your administrator identify opportunities to celebrate the successes of children and educators who are using AT well.

- Provide information about the AT skills that are needed in your district and suggest which staff members might need to have those skills.

- In consultation with the administrator, identify professional development topics and opportunities to provide it.

- Report to administrators when you observe situations where students are not making progress at the rate anticipated by the team when AT has been provided.

- Develop and implement a system to keep your administrator informed about which students have AT in their IEPs, what task the AT is supporting, and expected changes in student performance.

Advocacy and Program Improvement for AT Services

U se this chapter to look carefully at the coordinated set of services your program already provides and identify ways to improve and expand them.

✔ Advocate for AT services and resources at school board meetings, administrative staff meetings, community forums, parent organizations, and in professional organizations.

✔ Develop, implement, and monitor a long-range and systemwide AT plan.

✔ Use research-based program improvement strategies, including the Plan-Do-Study-Act cycle.

✔ Conduct ongoing evaluation of AT services in the same way as other services are evaluated

✔ Integrate AT into strategic plans, technology plans, and other improvement plans and policies to align efforts and leverage resources.

Administrators frequently have natural opportunities to advocate for AT in forums that are not open to teachers and others engaged more directly in the implementation of AT use. These forums may not even be open to AT program leaders. The opportunities occur at school board meetings, administrative staff meetings, community forums, parent-teacher organizations, and in administrators' professional organizations. Well-informed administrators who are aware of the AT use and AT needs of students can often take advantage of opportunities to integrate and improve AT services as their agency develops budgets, priorities, and lobbying efforts.

For example, administrators have the opportunity to ensure that AT needs are included in district or building technology plans and in the development of technology grants. In one school, a 21st Century Schools Grant provided AT for many students. One of the students commented at the end of the first year of the grant, "The other students thought I was dumb until they saw what I could write using voice recognition" (Polster & Katzmarek, 2004, p. 18). This ability to simply say, "Let's not forget the students who need assistive technology" is critical.

As administrators and AT leaders look for opportunities to enhance AT services by incorporating AT into grant and technology initiatives, they can also examine school improvement initiatives for the agency to determine ways that the use of AT might contribute to the achievement of agency-wide goals.

Improvements to the way AT services are delivered may be undertaken as part of a larger agency-wide improvement effort or as the result of a change in state or federal laws, new initiatives that are being implemented, or information gathered from self-assessments and surveys of consumers or providers. Program improvement entails change. Research into effective and sustainable change indicates that it can only be achieved when a concerned group of individuals struggles with tough decisions and arrives at potential solutions that reflect the current status of the school (Fullan, 2001). When a significant program change is desired, administrators cannot effectively dictate to staff members the specifics of what they need to do. Administrators can, however, convene a group of concerned individuals and make it possible for that group's members to participate in the decision making, planning, and implementation of program development and improvement activities.

Developing, Implementing, and Monitoring an AT Improvement Plan

As discussed in Chapter 2, "Leadership for AT Services," the development of a plan to improve AT services begins with development of a shared vision and shared agreement about the kind of changes that are needed to achieve that vision. The next step is to examine current practices to determine areas that need improvement. Two self-rating tools can be useful in this determination: (a) the "Education Tech Point Profile of AT Services in Schools" (Bowser & Reed, 2017), which is available as a free download at *www.educationtechpoints.org/manuals-materials* (see Appendix A); and (b) the Self-Evaluation Matrices for the Quality Indicators for Assistive Technology Services (QIAT Consortium, 2012), available as a free download at *qiat.org/indicators.html* (see Appendix B). Each person involved in the self-rating completes it, and results are compiled and reviewed by the planning group.

Whether school staff is using the Education Tech Point Profile of AT Services in Schools, the QIAT Self-Evaluation Matrices, or another AT program assessment tool, the self-assessment should be completed by a broad cross-section of the staff so that a comprehensive picture of strengths and weaknesses is obtained. If only a few individuals complete the self-assessment, it may present an incomplete or even inaccurate picture of the current services. For example, if only individuals knowledgeable about AT rate their own services, it will not reflect the experience of other educators throughout the district. Similarly, if only elementary school staff are involved in the assessment, it will not reflect the knowledge and skills of the middle and high school staff. AT leaders can be helpful in identifying individuals who will need to complete the self-assessment and disseminating the self-assessment tool to them.

Using the shared vision of what AT services should be and the results of the self-assessment, an administrator can bring together a group of people who will serve as a planning committee or task force. This small group of committed people will be the key to developing and implementing a plan for the shared vision. The AT planning committee should involve individuals with the authority and opportunity to make changes as well as those who have concern about the quality and availability of the existing services. Individuals to consider for this committee include the special education director, the technology coordinator, a building principal, a teacher, a therapist, supervisors of special services such as vision or hearing services or occupational and physical therapy, and a parent of a student who uses AT.

If the agency has a department that offers staff development, someone from that department could be included. Using the results of the self-assessment, the planning committee can begin to target areas of need and to meet those needs in a variety of appropriate ways. In addition to their specific job responsibilities, members of the group should be chosen for their connections to various groups within the school district and their ability to share information in ways that encourage interest and enthusiasm about AT throughout the agency. AT leaders can work with administrators to identify key people to serve on the planning committee and encourage them to participate.

One way of thinking about the membership of the AT planning group is offered by Gladwell (2002), who found that it takes three types of people to create successful change: Connectors, Mavens, and Salespeople. Connectors are people who are constantly bringing other people together and helping them see how they can help each other. Mavens are those individuals with great stores of knowledge in their field. Salespeople are those who can convince others that they "must" do something. The field of assistive technology has relied heavily on Mavens (e.g., AT experts). While their knowledge is certainly important, without Connectors and Salespeople, programs are less likely to experience successful and meaningful implementation and use of AT.

Administrators and AT leaders can work together to identify Connectors who can bring people together to share AT ideas and experiences. For example, when an occupational therapist works in multiple schools, she might notice that one teacher has been successful with integrating a student's use of an AAC device into classroom activities and arrange for a teacher who just got a new student with similar needs to visit the successful teacher's classroom. Even though the occupational therapist couldn't operate the AAC device herself, she saw the need for a connection between the two teachers.

An AT planning committee also needs members who are willing to "sell" the idea of AT use for students. Salespeople enthusiastically describe how good something is and how others should try it because it will help them address a problem they are experiencing. An AT planning committee member who acts as a salesperson might be the person who can make a presentation to the school board or a group of principals or teachers about how important AT is and how much difference it makes for individual students. In Gladwell's paradigm, Mavens are very knowledgeable but may make others feel intimidated by the scope of their knowledge.

Connectors and Salespeople are empowering. An effective AT planning committee will incorporate all three types of change makers.

Managing Change

Small changes, such as improving the way consideration or referral is addressed in a single building or a single program, may be accomplished in a few months with explanations at staff meetings and training where needed. The development of a new program or significant improvement in a larger program or across several settings will take more time and involve changes to the system itself. An example might be the change from an expert model of AT service delivery to a capacity building model, where many educators involved with a student have skills and abilities to take independent action when a student needs AT. Many school districts are undertaking this type of change as they realize that AT must be integrated into overall technology use by students.

Increasing skill levels of educators, and developing their view of the value of AT, requires training, practice, and coaching, as well as time to mature (Ashton, Lee, & Vega, 2005; Fixsen, Naoom, Blasé, Friedman, & Wallace, 2005). Throughout the process, the administrator or an assigned AT leader will oversee the activities of the planning group, provide reality checks about what is possible, establish schedules and timelines, and help prioritize. The AT leader will be most likely to provide suggestions for content of the procedural guidelines and job descriptions, perhaps even working with small groups as they develop draft proposals and will take the lead in organizing and providing training, including recruiting other AT personnel to help.

All individuals who will be involved in providing services in a new or revised model will need training and coaching on many topics, including the specific purpose and value of AT tools, the need for AT services to support those tools, the processes of consideration and assessment, the operation of specific tools, troubleshooting strategies, collection and use of meaningful data, and sources of technical assistance and support. Administrators will coordinate all aspects of the changes to make sure that the increments of the change are manageable. AT leaders will coach and mentor individuals as they implement new strategies.

Successful school improvement efforts require a dual focus on increasing individual service providers' capabilities and expanding the school district's or education agency's capacity to provide the service (Garmston & Wellman, 1995). To develop successful AT services, schools must focus on increasing the capabilities of the teachers and other service providers to make available effective AT services and a concurrent focus on specific changes that will expand the school district's capacity to provide those AT services. Changing the agency's capacity is accomplished by looking at the system and how it functions in relation to AT. Capacity building includes actions that have been discussed in more detail in other sections of this book and are addressed in many of the Quality Indicators, such as the following:

- developing written procedures that include AT and are widely disseminated to all staff,

- providing specific directions for dealing with requests for AT,

- developing forms to be used to request or provide AT devices and services,

- providing guidelines for including AT in the IEP, and

- planning for the acquisition of needed AT for both trials and ongoing use.

Whether making program-level changes in a single program or across a large school district, much can be learned from the research on improvement science (Langley et al., 2009). Improvement science holds that two different types of knowledge are needed to change how things are done: basic and profound knowledge. Basic knowledge comes from experimental research. Profound knowledge includes organization-specific knowledge about how things work in a particular setting or organization (Langley et al., 2009).

The core framework of improvement science is the plan-do-study-act cycle, a process for rapid cycles of learning from practice:

Plan: Using the information gathered from the self-assessment, target areas for improvement and develop a plan.

Do: Implement the plan.

Study: Check the results by reviewing progress made by students using AT and other data. Then seek input from participating staff.

Act: Make any changes needed based on the results. And repeat.

Improvement science can work at different levels of a school district for desired changes to be made by a team, a program, a school building, or an entire district.

Plan

USING THE PLAN-DO-STUDY-ACT PARADIGM AT ONE MIDDLE SCHOOL

The fifth/sixth-grade team at Jefferson Middle School had been concerned for some time about the performance of their students with disabilities on the state science tests. It had been the topic of discussion at many team meetings.

Last spring, Shalia Hawkins, the team leader, and two of the other teachers participated in a webinar about using text-to-speech to help students gain understanding of print materials. In addition, the whole school had reviewed the Quality Indicators for Assistive Technology Services and completed the self-assessment. They realized that they did not all know when students had AT in their IEPs and that they did not typically develop an implementation plan to document their responsibility to provide AT across all environments. They decided as a team to review IEPs for all students in their classrooms and develop implementation plans that they could review periodically to ensure that AT was being provided.

Do

Over the course of the next two months, they developed implementation plans for all 18 students with IEPs. They discovered that 12 of those students already had either AT for reading, or specifically text-to-speech in their IEPs. Although it was being implemented by the special education teacher, many of the content area teachers had not been aware of that requirement and had not been providing it. The media specialist agreed to take the lead in making sure that students had access to it in all classrooms and that the teachers were comfortable supporting its use. The special education teacher provided information on the students' ability to use the technology and their specific goals.

Study

At the end of the school year, Shalia asked the team to look at the test scores for the year and to specifically check to see whether the performance of the students using the text-to-speech to "read" their assignments had improved. They found that for 7 of the 12 students, there had been significant improvement in their performance on the science test. The other five had made slight improvements.

The team discussed the scores and decided to look more closely at the amount of time the students were using the text-to-speech and to ask the students what they thought about its use. They found that one student reported getting confused and not feeling comfortable using the text-to-speech. They worked with the special education teacher to provide more training on the use of text-to-speech. Two of the students said they didn't like using it because they felt "different." This led to an ongoing discussion about how to deal with the issue of not having the students who need text-to-speech be singled out. Two of the teachers decided to let any student who wanted to use text-to-speech go ahead and use it. They thought that would lessen the stigma.

Act

They all agreed that using text-to-speech was making a difference for the students about whom they were concerned. They planned to use it again in the fall with the planned changes.

Improvement science offers a practical approach to making change in service delivery in schools, including in the way AT services are delivered. Improvement science views variations as a source of ideas to improve programs and systems, rather than a problem to be eliminated. Implementation in new sites or when addressing a different type of AT or different age level need not be identical; in fact, success depends on unique knowledge-building systems because they promote motivation, ownership, and customization among the individuals implementing the new services (Lewis, 2015). Because providing AT services involves meeting the unique needs of each child as he or she grows, changes, and moves to new settings with different demands and characteristics, the flexibility offered by improvement science is valuable and practical.

As program improvement progresses, classroom teachers, related service personnel, paraprofessionals, and other support staff are well informed and collaborate to carry out the planned AT activities. Training is ongoing because not all staff will proceed at the same rate. Administrators and AT leaders will work together to monitor progress, identify roadblocks, and keep the program development on course. AT leaders will be instrumental in arranging, providing, and evaluating needed training and coaching.

A HELPFUL AT ADVISORY COMMITTEE

Fred Timm, Special Education Director, Stoughton (WI) School District

"The way AT services advanced in our district was through the very active advisory committee that the building principals supported. The committee set its goal of getting all special education teachers trained in the Wisconsin Assistive Technology Initiative (WATI) AT assessment system to develop a basic fluency when discussing students' AT needs with parents. That committee has brought to life the discussions of AT in the IEP meetings. While each of the school buildings within our district has an AT contact person, the main impetus has come from this very active advisory committee. There are 24 current members representing occupational therapy, physical therapy, speech language pathology, early childhood, regular education, and special education teachers from all grade levels.

"Although there are no building principals on the committee, they receive the minutes from each meeting and items from the advisory committee are discussed at the administrative council and building principal's meetings. (After all, they allocate the money.) The AT advisory committee has met about five times each school year during the last several years."

Ongoing Evaluation of AT Programs and Services

The ETP: Profile of AT Services in Schools or the Self-Evaluation Matrices for Quality Indicators for Assistive Technology Services can be used for ongoing evaluation. Both of these tools are useful for identifying a baseline, monitoring progress, and identifying areas of continued need.

Good program evaluation also includes the use of ongoing strategies to gain feedback from the consumers of the programs services, including the students, their families, and the general educators who are responsible for the student's daily educational program. Annual or semiannual surveys to determine both general satisfaction and specific needs can inform ongoing program development efforts.

The High Incidence Accessible Technology (HIAT) program at Montgomery County Public Schools in Maryland uses an exit interview after someone from the AT department has worked with a team to help a teacher try AT for a student with disabilities (DeCoste, personal communication, June 22, 2017). Questions they use include the following:

- What changed in your support to students?

  - AT strategies not implemented at this time,

  - AT trial strategies ineffective,

  - some trial strategies effective and implemented, or

  - all trial strategies effective and implemented.

- What aspect of student performance changed:

  - quality of work improved,

  - student is more independent with schoolwork,

  - student productivity increased,

  - student time on task increased, or

  - student motivation improved.

They also ask an open-ended question: What more could you and your team (including the AT support person) have done to help implement the use of AT?

Outreach

Advocating for AT often involves building a support network for an AT program through outreach. Outreach to other schools, programs, or departments often makes proactive systems change possible as opposed to a bits and pieces approach to problem solving. The University of Colorado at Boulder (Engage Program, 2017) defines the following five characteristics of outreach:

- collaboration with other groups,

- mutually beneficial partnership,

- grounded in evidence and scholarship,

- consistent with the mission of both groups, and

- catalyst for enhanced performance.

Outreach is seeing AT services in the context of a larger system and analyzing the roles of people who support AT use in a way that allows them to problem solve overriding issues and work with others with different perspectives. Outreach often requires that educators move out of their comfort zone and move toward shared collaboration and responsibility with people with whom they may not be used to interacting.

The results of outreach efforts are often more cost effective and efficient, and more satisfying to those involved. AT leaders are especially helpful in identifying the need for outreach to departments such as Information Technology Services or the Curriculum Adoption Department. But because administrators often interact with other department leaders, they are in a unique position to initiate outreach efforts, lead initial discussions, and identify resources that can be shared to enhance collaboration. Administrators can assign their staff members to outreach and collaboration activities and allocate time and resources to bring to the collaborative efforts.

Fred Timm, Special Education Director, Stoughton (WI) School District

"Joe and his AT leaders realized that the district's three-year goal to improve math scores on the state's high-stakes assessment provided them with an opportunity for collaboration. They reached out to the math curriculum director with a list of free and low-cost suggestions for technology applications that could help students learn new math skills and better demonstrate what they know. The Math department director provided funds for site licenses of some software applications, and together, the AT leader and the Math Department provided instruction to all educators about the district's math initiatives and the use of technology to support them. In the process, many students with disabilities benefited from the addition of potential AT solutions in their daily instructional programs."

JOE'S STORY: TARGETED APPLICATIONS

Integrating AT Throughout the Agency

AT can be addressed in many different areas, including improvement plans and grant applications as well as district-wide and curricular improvements. Once the vision of AT services is in place and the AT planning committee has developed a plan to move toward that vision, administrators can look for ways to integrate it into new and existing plans. For example, the building and district technology plan is an excellent place to include AT. Sometimes this opens the door to obtaining state and federal technology grants that can include some funding for AT through computer hardware and software with universal access features such as text-to-speech or voice recognition. These features benefit many students but are often identified as AT for some students with disabilities in the area of reading or writing.

Jane Jauquet, Director of Pupil Services, Wisconsin Rapids (WI) Public Schools

"I think the most important component of AT from an administrator's standpoint is to establish a systematic process for evaluating the need. The whole evaluation process should be completed with direct administrative input, support, and endorsement. I have designated a group of staff members who are assigned as a resource to each requested AT evaluation. These people go to AT training regularly to stay up to date. We also have a technology acquisition every fall where teachers can request hardware, software, updated programs, and peripherals for their classrooms. A team composed of me, the district technology director, and AT team members reviews the requests for appropriateness, compatibility with district systems, and duplication."

AT also can fit into existing overall school improvement plans. Anytime it is integrated into agency-wide activities, the likelihood of success increases. The more that implementers of plans are directly involved in the planning and decision-making process, the greater the likelihood of success.

Advocacy and Program Improvement: Getting Started

Actions related to program development center on the creation of a planning group, assessment of needs, and implementation of a plan for improvement.

Actions for Administrators

- Create a planning committee to identify program needs for AT.

- Complete a self-assessment.

- Work with the committee to develop a plan to improve AT services.

- Design a system to regularly evaluate AT services.

- Review strategic plans, technology plans, and other improvement plans and policies, looking for opportunities to align efforts and leverage resources.

Actions for AT Leaders

- Help identify individuals to serve on the planning committee.

- Help disseminate and collect self-assessments.

- Help review and analyze self-assessment data.

- Participate in developing, implementing, and monitoring the AT improvement plan.

CHAPTER 6

Planning Your AT Leadership

Use this chapter to make a personal plan for enhancing AT services that your agency provides.

- ✔ Rate your own AT leadership skills and identify two or three skill areas that you would like to improve.

- ✔ Work with AT leaders in your agency to develop an AT planning group.

- ✔ Use a rating instrument to assess your current AT service design and identify areas in need of improvement.

- ✔ Develop a 3-year plan for enhancing AT services in your agency.

At the beginning of this book, we identified goals for our work together. We hoped that you would be able to:

- identify ways that you can directly support educational programs that encourage and sustain students' and educators' use of AT;

- create and share a vision of your agency's approach to providing AT devices and services;

- manage material resources, allocation of personnel, time, and physical resources in a way that helps to provide an efficient, ethical, and cost-effective system for AT;

- support educators in learning and applying pedagogical strategies for integrating the use of AT into the educational programs of students with disabilities; and

- regularly assess current AT services and identify strategies to improve the current model.

The Leadership Self-Rating (Table 6.1) provides a way to help you analyze where you are in reaching these goals and give direction for your personal journey of leading your district or program to excellence in AT services. It can help you identify your strengths and the places where you will want to focus your attention. Use 1 = initial AT efforts *to* 4 = consistently addressed.

TABLE 6.1.

AT Leadership Self-Rating

LEADERSHIP FOR AT SERVICES	SELF-RATING			
Know what AT is and how it can benefit students with disabilities.	1	2	3	4
Know who the AT leaders are in the agency and work with them directly to develop, maintain, and improve AT services.	1	2	3	4
Know the legal definitions of AT, the requirements to provide AT for students with disabilities, and the implications for my program.	1	2	3	4
Help staff, students, and families develop a vision for AT use and communicate that vision widely.	1	2	3	4
Support faculty and staff in using AT to improve the education of students with disabilities.	1	2	3	4
Develop a culture where AT devices and services are valued and used.	1	2	3	4
Facilitate and support collaboration between departments to improve learning for student with disabilities through the use of AT.	1	2	3	4
Ensure equity of access to AT devices and services for students of all ages, disabilities, and school placements.	1	2	3	4
MANAGEMENT FOR AT SERVICES	**SELF-RATING**			
Develop, implement, and monitor policies and written operating guidelines for providing AT services.	1	2	3	4
Ensure that written guidelines include processes for AT consideration during the IEP meeting, AT assessment, and implementation of AT plans.	1	2	3	4
Ensure that all appropriate employees know how to respond to a parent's request for AT.	1	2	3	4
Require that staff use data to make AT decisions.	1	2	3	4
Make available planning time, funds, and human resources for the provision of AT services.	1	2	3	4
Upgrade the AT inventory as needed.	1	2	3	4
Monitor AT services to ensure they are provided in a cost-effective and efficient manner.	1	2	3	4

(continued next page)

SUPERVISION FOR AT SERVICES	SELF-RATING			
Assess staff AT knowledge, skills, performance, and training needs.	1	2	3	4
Recruit individuals with AT skills.	1	2	3	4
Ensure that all staff, including general education teachers, have the necessary understanding of AT to fulfill their role in supporting the use of AT by students with disabilities in their classes.	1	2	3	4
Demonstrate interest and support for making AT available and usable by students as part of staff evaluation and supervision.	1	2	3	4
Ensure that all staff members who serve a child with a disability implement the IEP, including any use of AT, in a legal and ethical manner.	1	2	3	4
Foster a school environment that has a low level of conflict and assist in conflict resolution, including conflict about AT.	1	2	3	4
Support teams as they work to make AT available to students with disabilities by providing structure and clear expectations.	1	2	3	4
ADVOCACY AND PROGRAM IMPROVEMENT FOR AT SERVICES	SELF-RATING			
Advocate for AT services and resources at school board meetings, administrative staff meetings, community forums, parent organizations, and professional organizations.	1	2	3	4
Develop, implement, and monitor a long-range and system-wide AT plan.	1	2	3	4
Use research-based program improvement strategies, including the Plan-Do-Study-Act cycle.	1	2	3	4
Conduct ongoing evaluation of AT services in the same way as other services are evaluated.	1	2	3	4
Integrate AT into strategic plans, technology plans, and other improvement plans and policies to align efforts and leverage resources.	1	2	3	4

Some administrators and AT leaders, after reading to this point, may be asking themselves questions such as "Why an AT focus for me?" "Why administrators and AT leaders?" or "What needs to be done?" This final chapter will address those questions and provide meaningful answers.

"Why an AT Focus for Me?": Reaffirming the Value of AT Planning

We have a shared goal of helping all students learn and demonstrate what they have learned in order to make progress in the curriculum. Research shows AT makes a difference in the performance of students with disabilities. It allows them to better demonstrate their skills and knowledge and to make greater progress in the curriculum. To make this kind of progress, they need access to AT for the tasks with which they struggle, and that access must include daily opportunities to use the AT for meaningful tasks.

Initial access to AT can be provided by an AT team or an AT specialist working with the student-centered team to select and acquire the AT. But opportunities for meaningful *use* of the AT can only be provided by the staff in the student's classroom, not by specialists who have infrequent direct contact with a student. To be successful, AT use must be timely, spontaneous, and an integral part of the student's education.

High-stakes assessment and the ESSA's focus on school improvement have made it critical to address the needs of struggling students and students with disabilities in order to show adequate yearly progress for the school as a whole. School districts as well as state and federal governments are closely examining aggregate achievement scores of all students in a district as well as the scores of groups such as English language learners and students with disabilities.

Particularly when the scores of students with disabilities such as specific learning disabilities or dyslexia are considered, the use of AT can help such students to show an increase of several percentile points on annual assessments. AT used daily in a classroom setting overcomes barriers to learning. Even when a student's AT is not allowable on a state assessment, the enhanced learning that results from daily AT use is evident in student scores on state and district assessments.

For example, Stodden, Roberts, Takahishi, Park, and Stodden (2012) found that the use of text-to-speech software (a) increases vocabulary; (b) increases reading speed; (c) provides exposure to correct pronunciation; (d) allows more room in active memory for constructing meaning from text; and (e) leaves students less fatigued. If a student is able to focus on content of the science chapter rather than struggling to decode the text, he is able to learn more.

"Why Administrators *and* AT Leaders?": Making a Difference in AT Programs

My conclusion from this evidence, as a whole, is that leadership has very significant effects on the quality of the school organization and on student learning. As far as I am aware, there is not a single documented case of a school successfully turning around its student achievement trajectory in the absence of talented leadership. One explanation for this is that leadership serves as a catalyst for unleashing the potential capacities that already exist in the organization. Those in leadership roles have a tremendous responsibility to "get it right." Fortunately, we know a great deal about what getting it right means. (Leithwood, 2006, p. 182)

Principals and other educational leaders have the power to initiate change (Fullan, 2001). They can nurture a supportive culture for change and involve key teachers who exert influence over their colleagues (Marzano, Waters, & McNulty, 2005; Rogers, 2003).

There is a common core of successful leadership practices ("the basics") that all good leaders master. Flexibility, which is noted by improvement science as a critical component to successful change, entails adapting these core practices to the unique circumstances in which leaders find themselves. Effective leaders emphasize the priority they attach to achievement and instruction, provide targeted and phased focus for school improvement efforts, and work to build cooperative working relationships among those they lead (Leithwood, 2008).

Leadership effects are usually largest where they are needed most (Leithwood, 2008). If your AT program is new or if the self-assessments you complete at the district level indicate that significant changes are needed, the leadership provided by administrators and AT leaders will figure strongly in the potential for improvement.

Good leadership responds to the unique features found in the organization. In a small school district, an administrator for an AT program may actually be a member of an AT planning committee and help to write operating guidelines along with AT leaders. In a larger district, specific AT planning activities may be assigned to others and submitted to administrators for approval. With changing demands and circumstances, flexibility is a prerequisite for good leadership (Yukl & Lepsinger, 2004).

Planning AT Leadership: Getting Started

When leaders include teachers and other stakeholders in developing a shared vision and goals for reaching the vision, their actions give meaning, a common purpose, challenge, and motivation to everyone in the school (Bass & Avolio 1994; Marzano et al., 2005; Schmoker 1999; Senge et al., 1999).

We have presented the Education Tech Points: Profile of AT Services in Schools and the Self-Evaluation Matrices for Quality Indicators for Assistive Technology Services as self-ratings that can provide the information necessary to help agencies develop a vision.

However, administrators and AT leaders often need to develop their own visions of how they will proceed at the district level before initiating leadership activities. The AT Leadership Self-Rating tool presented earlier was developed to provide a structure for this kind of planning for school administrator and AT leaders.

An earlier version of the AT Leadership Self-Rating was developed to help administrators reflect on their role in supporting and developing AT programs (Bowser & Reed, 2004). Using it, McMahon (2005) surveyed school principals in Virginia and found that although many reported carrying out several of the activities included in the self-rating, few included AT in their recruiting or evaluation of teachers. Surveying a broader range of administrators in Oregon, including special education directors as well as principals, Schechla-Ferris (2009) found that 68% of participants reported that they did not include AT service delivery as part of staff evaluation or supervision. Schechla-Ferris (2009) concluded that without AT knowledge and skills being part of the teacher evaluation process, it is difficult for school leaders to make improvements in the quality or availability of AT services. In this publication, the content of the self-assessment has been updated to reflect new information about the roles of school administrators and other leaders in school improvement efforts.

Actions for Administrators

- Use the AT Leadership Self-Rating tool to rate your own AT leadership efforts. Invite other AT leaders in your program(s) to rate their efforts.

- Use the information gained from the compiled self-rating to make a personal action plan.

Actions for AT Leaders

- Work with your administrator to review the results of the Leadership Self- Rating.

- Using the information gained, make a personal action plan.

• • •

Best wishes for an exciting and fruitful AT Leadership journey. We know that you will encounter many talented and dedicated AT leaders as you work to develop and improve your AT services.

Throughout this book we have included many suggestions, ideas, and examples. We have many more. If you want more information or simply want to have a conversation about how to get started, here is how to find us: Gayl Bowser at *gaylbowser@gmail.com* and Penny Reed at *1happypenny@gmail.com*.

References

Alnahdi, G. (2014). Assistive technology in special education and the universal design for learning. *Turkish Online Journal of Education Technology, 13*(2), 18–23.

Americans with Disabilities Act of 1990, Publ. No. 101-336, 104 Stat. 328. 1990.

Ash, R., & Persall, M. (2007). "Formative leadership" theory views principal as leader of leaders. Retrieved from *www.educationworld.com/a_issues/chat/chat025.shtml*

Ashton, T., Lee, Y., & Vega, L. A. (2005). Assistive technology: Perceived knowledge, attitudes, and challenges of AT use in special education. *Journal of Special Education Technology, 20*(2), 60–63.

Bagnato, S. J., Neisworth, J. T., & Pretti-Frontczak, K. (2010). *Linking authentic assessment and early childhood intervention: Best measures for best practices* (2nd ed.). Baltimore, MD: Brookes Publishing.

Bass, B. M., & Avolio, B. J. (1994). *Improving organizational effectiveness through transformational leadership.* Thousand Oaks, CA: Sage.

Bateman, D., & Bateman, C. F. (2001). *A principal's guide to special education.* Arlington, VA: Council for Exceptional Children.

Behrmann, M. M., & Schepis, M. M. (1994). Assistive technology assessment: A multiple case study of three approaches with students with physical disabilities during the transition from school to work. *Journal of Vocational Rehabilitation, 4* (3), 202–210.

Blase, J., & Blase, J. (2001). The teacher's principal. *Journal of Staff Development, 22*(1), 22–25.

Bottos, M., Bolcati, C., Sciuto, L., Ruggeri, C., & Feliciangeli, A. (2001). Powered wheelchairs and independence in young children with tetraplegia. *Developmental Medicine and Child Neurology, 43,* 769–777.

Bouck, E. (2106). A national snapshot of assistive technology for students with disabilities. *Journal of Special Education Technology, 31*(1).

Bowser, G. (Ed.). (2003). *Assistive technology model operating guidelines for school districts and IEP teams.* Roseburg, OR: Oregon Technology Access Program. Retrieved from *www.douglasesd.k12.or.us/otap/publications*

Bowser, G. & Reed, P. (1995). Education tech points for assistive technology planning. *Journal of Special Education Technology, 7*(4), 325–338.

Bowser, G., & Reed, P. (1998). *Education tech points: A framework for assistive technology planning.* Roseburg, OR: Coalition for Assistive Technology in Oregon.

Bowser, G., & Reed, P. (2004). *A school administrator's desktop guide to assistive technology.* Reston, VA: Technology and Media Division of the Council for Exceptional Children.

Bowser, G., & Reed, P. (2012). *Education tech points: A framework for assistive technology planning* (3rd ed.). Roseburg, OR: Coalition for Assistive Technology in Oregon.

Bowser, G., & Reed, P. (2017). Education Tech Points: Profile of AT Services in Schools. Winchester, OR: Coalition for Assistive Technology in Oregon. Retrieved from *www.educationtechpoints.org/manuals-materials*

Brewer, H. (2001). Ten steps to success. *Journal of Staff Development, 22*(1), 30–31.

Browder, D. M., Wood, L., Thompson, J., & Ribuffo, C. (2014). Innovation configuration: Evidence-based practices for students with severe disabilities. CEEDAR Document No. IC-3, pp. 36–38. Gainesville, FL: CEEDAR Center.

Butler, J. A. (1992). Staff development. *School Improvement Research Series, 12.*

Cuban, L. (1986). *Teachers and machines.* New York, NY: Teachers College Press.

Cullen, J., Richards, S. B., & Lawless-Frank, C. (2008). Using software to enhance the writing skills of students with special needs. *Journal of Special Education Technology, 23*(2), 33–43.

DeCoste, D. (2017). Personal communication.

DeCoste, D., & Bowser, G. (2016). *The evolution of AT teams: Redesigning your AT services.* Orlando, FL: Assistive Technology Industries Association Conference, January 2016.

DeCoste, D., Reed, P., & Kaplan, M. (2005). *Assistive technology teams: Many ways to do it well.* National Assistive Technology in Education (NATE) Network. Retrieved from *www.natenetwork.org*

Dell, A. G., Newton, D. A., & Petroff, J. G. (2008). *Assistive technology in the classroom: Enhancing the school experiences of students with disabilities.* Upper Saddle River, NJ: Pearson Education.

Delaney, E. (1999). Curriculum and intervention strategies (PowerPoint presentation). Presented at University of Illinois, Chicago.

Duhigg, C., (2016, February 28), What Google learned from its quest to build the perfect team. *New York Times Magazine.* Retrieved from *www.nytimes.com/2016/02/28/magazine/what-google-learned-from-its-quest-to-build-the-perfect-team.html*

Engage Program (2017). Our values. Boulder, CO: University of Colorado. Retrieved from *www.colorado.edu/cuengage/about-us#equity*

Fennema-Jansen, S. (2001). Measuring effectiveness: Technology to support writing. *Special Education Technology Practice, 3*(1), 16–22.

Fixsen, D. L., Naoom, S. F., Blasé, K. A., Friedman, R. M., & Wallace, F. (2005). *Implementation research: A synthesis of the literature*. Tampa, FL: National Implementation Research Network, University of South Florida.

Fullan, M. (2001). *Leading in a culture of change*. San Francisco, CA: Jossey-Bass.

Gajria, M., Jitendra, A. K., Sood, S., & Sacks, G. (2007). Improving comprehension of expository text in students with LD: A research synthesis. *Journal of Learning Disabilities, 40*, 210–225.

Garmston, R. & Wellman, B., (1995). Adaptive schools in a quantum universe. *Educational Leadership, 52*(7), 6–12.

Gladwell, M. (2002). *The tipping point*. Boston, MA: Back Bay Books.

Greenberg, J., & Baron, R. A. (2000). *Behavior in organizations* (7th ed.). Upper Saddle River, NJ: Prentice Hall.

Hall, T. and Strangman, N. (2002). *Graphic organizers*. Wakefield, MA: National Center on Accessing the General Curriculum.

Hasselbring, T. S., & Glaser, C. H. (2000). Use of computer technology to help students with special needs. *Future of Children, 10*(2), 102–122.

Heathfield, S. (2017). 12 tips for teambuilding in the workplace. Retrieved from *www.thebalance.com/tips-for-team-building-1918512*

Howe, A. (2017, March 23). Opinion analysis: Court's decision rejecting low bar for students with disabilities, under the spotlight. SCOTUSblog. Retrieved from *www.scotusblog.com/2017/03/opinion-analysis-courts-decision-rejecting-low-bar-students-disabilities-spotlight*

Individuals with Disabilities Education Improvement Act of 2004 (IDEA), P.L. 108-446. 20 U.S.C. § 1401 et seq.; 34 C.F.R. § 300.1 et seq.

Johnstone, C., Thurlow, M., Altman, J., Timmons, J. & Kato, K. (2009). Assistive technology approaches for large-scale assessment: Perceptions of teachers of students with visual impairments. *Exceptionality, 17*(2), 66–75.

Jones, M. A., McEwen, I. R., & Hansen, L. (2003). Use of power mobility for a young child with spinal muscular atrophy. *Physical Therapy, 83*, 253–262.

Joyce, B., & Showers, B. (2002). *Student achievement through staff development* (3rd ed.). Alexandria, VA: Association for Supervision and Curriculum Development.

Judge, S. L. (2000). Accessing and funding assistive technology for young children with disabilities. *Early Childhood Education Journal, 28*(2), 125–131.

Judge, S. & Simms, K. A. (2009). Assistive technology training at the pre-service level: A national snapshot of teacher preparation programs. *Teacher Education and Special Education, 32*(1), 33–44.

Langley, G. J., Moen, R. D., Nolan, K. M., Nolan, T. W., Norman, C. L. & Provost, L. P. (2009). *The improvement guide.* San Francisco, CA: Jossey-Bass.

Leggett, W .P. & Persichitte, K. A. (1998). Cited in LumberJack Leadership: School Administrators and Technology Integration. Retrieved from *http://eduscapes.com/sessions/lumber/lumber3.htm*

Leithwood, K. (2006). The 2005 Willower Family Lecture: Leadership according to the evidence. *Leadership and Policy in Schools, 5,*177–202.

Leithwood, K. (2008). Transformational leadership for challenging schools. *Orbit, 37*(2 & 3), 110–112.

Leithwood, K., Harris, A., and D. Hopkins. (2008). Seven strong claims about successful school leadership. *School Leadership & Management 28*(1), 27-42.

Lewis, C. (2015). What is improvement science? Do we need it in education? *Educational Researcher, 44*(1), 54–61.

MacArthur, C. A., & Cavalier, A. R. (2004). Dictation and speech recognition technology as test accommodations. *Exceptional Children, 71*(1), 43–58.

Marzano, R. J., Waters, T., & McNulty, B. A. (2005). *School leadership that works: From research to results.* Alexandria, VA: Association for Supervision and Curriculum Development.

Mascall, B., & Leithwood, K. (2008). The effects of total leadership on student learning. *Educational Administration Quarterly, 44*(4), 529–561.

McCollum, D., Nation, S., & Gunn, S. (2014). The effects of a speech-to-text software application on written expression for students with various disabilities. *National Forum of Special Education Journal, 25*(1), 1–13.

McGivern, J. E., & McKevitt, B. C. (2002). Best practices in working with students using assistive technology. *Best Practices in School Psychology IV, 1,* 1537–1553.

McInerney, M., Osher, D., & Kane, M. (1997). *Improving the availability and use of technology for children with disabilities: Final report.* Washington, DC: Chesapeake Institute of the American Institutes for Research.

McMahon, P. J. (2005). Special education assistive technology: A phenomenological study of building administrator knowledge and practices. Ph.D. thesis, The College of William and Mary. Retrieved from *www.learntechlib.org/p/128507/*

Millar, D., Light, J. C., & Schlosser, R. W., (2006). The impact of augmentative and alternative communication intervention on the speech production of individuals with developmental disabilities: A research review. *Journal of Speech, Language, and Hearing Research, 49*(2), 248–264.

Miller, V. (2003). Summary of complaint proceedings. Presentation at Council of Oregon School Administrators Conference, Eugene, OR.

Murphy, C. U., & Lick, D. W. (2001). The principal as study group leader. *Journal of Staff Development, 22*(1), 37–38.

National Task Force on Technology and Disability. (2004). *Within our reach: Findings and recommendations of the National Task Force on Technology and Disability.* Flint, MI: The Disability Network.

Neufeld, B. & Roper, D. (2003). *Coaching: A strategy for developing instructional capacity,* Annenberg Institute for School Reform, Washington, DC.

Northouse, P. G. (2016). *Leadership theory and practice* (7th ed.). Thousand Oaks, CA: Sage Publications.

Office of Educational Technology. (2017). *National Education Technology Plan.* Retrieved from *https://tech.ed.gov/netp/*

Parsons, R. B. (2001). Ten principles for principals. *Principal, 80*(4), 49–51.

Polster, C. & Katzmarek, J. (2004). Using assistive technology to support struggling readers and writers. *Closing the Gap, 22*(6), 18.

QIAT Consortium. (2012). Self-Evaluation Matrices for Quality Indicators for Assistive Technology Services. Retrieved from *www.qiat.org/indicators.html*

QIAT Leadership Team. (2015). *Quality indicators for assistive technology: A comprehensive guide to assistive technology services.* Wakefield, MA: CAST Professional Publishing.

Quinlan, T. (2004). Speech recognition technology and students with writing difficulties: Improving fluency. *Journal of Educational Psychology*, 96(2), 337.

Reed, P., Bowser, G., & Korsten, J. (2002). *How do you know it? How can you show it?* Oshkosh, WI: Wisconsin Assistive Technology Initiative. Retrieved from *https://wilmuedt6035.pbworks.com/f/at%20know%20it%20show%20it.pdf*

Rehabilitation Act of 1973, Section 504, P.L. 93-112, 29 U.S.C. § 794. 1977.

Rogers, E. M. (2003). *Diffusion of innovations* (5th ed.). New York: Free Press.

Sam, H. D., Othman, A., & Nordin, Z. S. (2005). Computer self-efficacy, computer anxiety, and attitudes toward the Internet: A study among undergraduates in Unimas. *Educational Technology and Society, 8*(4), 205–219.

Schechla-Ferris, E .J. (2009). A reliability and validity study of the self-assessment component of the administrator's desktop guide to assistive technology. Minneapolis, MN: Capella University. Unpublished doctoral dissertation.

Schepis, M. M., Reid, D., Behrmann, M., & Sutton, K. (1998). Increasing communicative interactions of young children with autism using voice output communication aid and naturalistic teaching. *Journal of Applied Behavior Analysis, 31*(4), 561–578.

Scherer, M. (2000). *Living in the state of stuck: How assistive technology impacts the lives of people with disabilities.* Cambridge, MA: Brookline Books/Lumen Editions.

Schmoker, M. (1999). *Results: The key to continuous school improvement.* Alexandria, VA: Association for Supervision and Curriculum Development.

Senge, P., Kleiner, A., Roberts, C., Ross, R., Roth, G., & Smith, B. (1999). *The dance of change.* New York, NY: Random House.

Siegenthaler, E., Wurtz, P., & Groner, R. (2011). Improving the usability of e-book readers. *Journal of Usability Studies, 6*(1), 25–38.

Silió, M. C., & Barbetta, P. M. (2010). The effects of word prediction and text-to-speech technologies on the narrative writing skills of Hispanic students with specific learning disabilities. *Journal of Special Education Technology, 25*(4), 17–32.

Spooner, F., Browder, D. M., & Mims, P. (2011). Sensory, physical, and healthcare needs. In D. M. Browder & F. Spooner (Eds.), *Teaching students with moderate and severe disabilities* (pp. 241–261). New York, NY: Guilford.

Stodden, R. A., Roberts, K. D., Takahashi, K., Park, H. J. & Stodden, N. J. (2012). Use of text-to-speech software to improve reading skills of high school struggling readers. *Procedia Computer Science, 14,* 359–362.

Tam, C., Archer, J., Mays, J., & Skidmore, G. (2005). Measuring the outcomes of word cueing technology. *Canadian Journal of Occupational Therapy, 72*(5), 301–308.

Technology Standards for School Administrators Collaborative. (2001). *Technology standards for school administrators.* Retrieved from *www.orlandodiocese.org/wp-content/uploads/2012/07/Administrators_Standards.pdf*

Truesdale, W. T. (2003). The implementation of peer coaching on the transferability of staff development to classroom practice in two selected Chicago public elementary schools. *Dissertation Abstracts International, 64*(1), 3923.

Turner, C. & McCarthy, G. (2015). Coachable moments: Identifying factors that influence managers to take advantage of coachable moments in day-to-day management. *International Journal of Evidence-Based Coaching and Mentoring, 113*(1), 1–13.

Uben, L., & Hughes, L. (1997). *The principal.* Needham Heights, MA: Allyn and Bacon.

U.S. Department of Justice and U.S. Department of Education. (2014). Dear Colleague Letter from the Active Assistant Attorney General for Civil Rights, U.S. Department of Justice, the Acting Assistant Secretary Office of Special Education and Rehabilitative Services, U.S. Department of Education and the Assistant Secretary, Office of Civil Rights, U.S. Department of Education of Effective Communication–November 12, 2014. Retrieved from *www2.ed.gov/about/offices/list/ocr/letters/colleague-effective-communication-201411.pdf*

Watson, A. H., Ito, M., Smith, R. O., & Andersen, L. T. (2010). Effect of assistive technology in a public school setting. *American Journal of Occupational Therapy 64*(1), 18–29.

Wood, S. G., Moxley, J. H., Tighe, E. L., & Wagner, R. K. (2018). Does use of text-to-speech and related read-aloud tools improve reading comprehension for students with reading disabilities? A meta-analysis. *Journal of Learning Disabilities 51*(1), 73–84.

Yukl, G., & Lepsinger, L. (2004). *Flexible leadership: Creating value by balancing multiple challenges and choices.* San Francisco, CA: Jossey and Bass.

Zabala, J. (2007). Development and evaluation of quality indicators for assistive technology services. University of Kentucky Doctoral Dissertations, Paper 517. Retrieved from *http://uknowledge.uky.edu/gradschool_diss/517*

Zimmerman, J. (2006). Why some teachers resist change and what principals can do about it. *NASSP Bulletin, 90*(3), 238–249.

Education Tech Points: Profile of AT Services in Schools

COMPONENTS OF EFFECTIVE ASSISTIVE TECHNOLOGY SERVICE DELIVERY	HIGHLY SATISFACTORY		VARIATIONS		NEEDS IMPROVEMENT
	(5)	(4)	(3)	(2)	(1)
1. CONSIDERATION AND REFERRAL					
A. School district provides training about AT, legal mandates, and what AT can do for students with disabilities.	All staff, including regular educators, are aware of AT, have received training, and can contribute to team's consideration of AT.	Most special and regular educators are aware of AT, have received training, and can contribute to team's consideration of AT.	Some special and regular educators are aware of AT, have received training, and can contribute to team's consideration of AT.	A few special educators are aware of AT and have received some training. Consideration is inconsistent.	Staff members have not received training about AT. AT is often dismissed without discussion during the IEP meeting.
B. School district special education procedure manual or teacher handbook includes AT devices and services.	Procedure manual has clear, specific directions and procedures for providing AT devices and services.	Procedure manual has directions for providing AT devices and services.	Procedure manual has a few directions for AT devices and services, but they are not sufficient.	Procedure manual mentions AT but lacks specific guidance.	There is no procedure manual, or the existing manual does not mention AT.
C. School district forms/reports include places to request and describe AT.	All appropriate forms include clearly identifiable places to indicate and describe AT devices and/or services.	District forms mention AT but do not provide a way to clearly describe AT devices and/ or services discussed.	Forms do not encourage mention of AT, but assessment and progress reports sometimes describe it.	School district forms do not mention AT and reports do not address AT.	Staff members are not encouraged or directed to consider AT.

(continued next page)

COMPONENTS OF EFFECTIVE ASSISTIVE TECHNOLOGY SERVICE DELIVERY	HIGHLY SATISFACTORY		VARIATIONS		NEEDS IMPROVEMENT
	(5)	(4)	(3)	(2)	(1)
D. District promotes parent participation in all aspects of AT decision making and use.	Parents are routinely included in AT decision making and planning for trials and ongoing use.	Parents are often part of the AT decision-making process and planning for trials and ongoing use.	District has procedures to solicit parent input but no participation in AT decisions.	Parents are informed about decisions after they are made or are minimally involved.	Parent AT inquiries are handled individually. There is no process to include parents.
2. EVALUATION					
A. Student-centered teams match student needs, abilities, environments, and tasks to appropriate tools.	Student-centered teams have the training, time, resources, and support needed to match tools to student AT needs.	Teams generally match student needs, abilities, environments, and tasks to appropriate tools.	Teams understand the need to match student needs to appropriate tools but lack resources or support.	Teams have limited ability to match student needs to appropriate tools.	Little or no AT available. Teams do not attempt to match student needs to appropriate AT tools.
B. Student-centered teams use a clearly defined decision-making process for AT.	Team members are trained in, and use, a clearly defined decision-making process.	Team members are trained and are making progress in using a clearly defined decision-making process.	Most team members are trained and teams sometimes use a clearly defined decision-making process.	Some team members are trained, but teams rarely use an organized decision-making process.	Team members do not use a decision-making process.
C. During special education eligibility evaluation or re-evaluation, AT is used as indicated in current IEP or as needed.	Eligibility evaluators know about and use a variety of AT during eligibility evaluations.	Evaluators are trained about some aspects of AT and use it with students as indicated during eligibility evaluations.	Evaluators are trained about some types of AT but inconsistently use it with students during eligibility evaluations.	Eligibility evaluators have some training in AT and how to utilize it in evaluations.	Eligibility evaluators are not knowledgeable about AT, and it is not used during evaluations.
D. Teams refer a student for evaluation from persons with additional expertise in AT when needed.	Referrals supplement information gathered by staff. They are timely and tailored to student needs.	Referrals replace local evaluation in areas where staff do not have sufficient information.	Referrals to individuals with additional AT expertise are used inconsistently.	Referrals for additional AT expertise are occasionally made but not tailored to student needs.	Referrals for additional AT expertise are never made.
3. TRIAL PERIODS					
A. School district has an effective system for child-specific teams to obtain AT for trial periods.	Child-centered teams routinely obtain AT for trial use.	Child-centered teams often obtain AT for trial use.	Child-centered teams occasionally arrange for a loan of AT for a trial.	Individuals sometimes arrange AT trials.	Trial periods are not implemented.

(continued next page)

COMPONENTS OF EFFECTIVE ASSISTIVE TECHNOLOGY SERVICE DELIVERY	HIGHLY SATISFACTORY		VARIATIONS		NEEDS IMPROVEMENT
	(5)	(4)	(3)	(2)	(1)
B. Teams design and carry out trial periods that include the goal for AT use, location of trials, expected outcomes, and person responsible.	Child-centered teams routinely develop written plans for AT trials that include all relevant aspects.	Child-centered teams usually develop written plans for AT trials that include all relevant aspects.	Trial periods are generally used but may lack the quality and consistency necessary to answer questions about AT use.	Trials are conducted inconsistently across the district.	AT devices are frequently acquired without any trial period to determine a student's need and ability to use them.
C. Data collected from the trial period are used to make decisions about the child's need for AT.	Child-centered teams collect results data according to a well-designed plan and consistently use it.	Child-centered teams usually collect and use results data according to a plan.	Teams regularly plan for data collection but often do not adjust plan in response to data.	Data are often not sufficient due to lack of clear plan for collection and use.	Data are not collected or used in making decisions about AT.
4. PLAN DEVELOPMENT					
A. District's IEPs include AT devices/ services in ways that are clear and understandable to everyone.	IEPs include AT in ways that clearly reflect its use (e.g., goals, related services, supplementary aids and services).	IEPs usually include AT and/ or reflect that AT was considered.	IEPs generally include AT but show lack of understanding (e.g., AT listed as accommodation, but AT Consideration says "No").	AT is inconsistently written into IEPs and/or described in ways that are unclear or confusing.	AT is never or rarely included in IEPs.
B. School district assures staff are trained in how to effectively write AT into IEPs when needed.	All staff members have received training to effectively write AT into IEPs.	Most staff members have received training in writing AT into IEPs.	Some staff members have been trained in writing AT into IEPs.	Few staff members have been trained in writing AT into IEPs, and training is inconsistently applied.	No specific training has been provided.
C. IEP teams, including parents, design and write integrated, collaborative IEPs that incorporate AT appropriately.	IEP teams that include parents develop IEPs collaboratively that integrate AT into the educational program.	Parents have input, and staff cooperatively write child-centered IEPs that integrate AT into the educational program.	IEPs are not consistently written collaboratively and may not show the integration of AT into the educational program.	Individuals write IEP objectives that include AT, with some attempt to coordinate during the IEP meeting.	Individuals write IEP objectives that include AT based only on what they see within their own disciplines.

(continued next page)

COMPONENTS OF EFFECTIVE ASSISTIVE TECHNOLOGY SERVICE DELIVERY	HIGHLY SATISFACTORY		VARIATIONS		NEEDS IMPROVEMENT
	(5)	(4)	(3)	(2)	(1)
5. IMPLEMENTATION					
A. All team members collaborate to ensure that a plan for AT use is developed and implemented.	Team members define shared responsibilities to implement IEP together through an AT implementation plan.	Team members develop an AT implementation plan together.	Team members generally share AT implementation responsibilities.	Implementation occurs in most settings for most activities, but responsibility is not shared.	Implementation is inconsistent, often falling on one person.
B. Clear responsibility for training, equipment maintenance, and operation assigned to specific staff members.	Team members know their responsibilities, work together to train others, keep equipment working, and ensure its use across environments.	Team members generally know their roles. Equipment is operating and in use in most cases, and some training is provided.	One or two staff members are viewed as being responsible for AT, and little training of others is provided.	Some equipment is not working appropriately. Responsibility for implementation is vague and training is not provided.	Equipment is typically unused, underused, or not working due to confusion about roles and responsibilities.
C. School district has a budget for the purchase of AT.	AT is included in the district budget with sufficient funding to acquire/maintain an array of AT needed.	AT is included in the district budget that generally meets the need for items for specific students.	AT is included in the district budget but does not meet the identified student's needs.	AT is not in the budget, but items are sometimes purchased when needed.	AT is never purchased by the district.
D. Team members involved in the provision of AT services have time to meet together.	Regular meeting times are scheduled for teams to discuss AT implementation.	Team members have some scheduled times to discuss AT.	Some team members meet, but not all can attend meetings.	Occasional meetings to discuss AT occur.	Staff members do not have time or opportunity to talk to each other about AT.
E. Identified consultant(s) from within or outside the district help personnel working with students using AT.	Uniformly understood procedures support AT specialist or team to provide training and technical assistance.	Consultant or team is regularly available for AT activities: evaluations, consultations, training, and follow-up.	Consultant or team has regular schedule for AT duties. Part-time AT members called on as time permits.	AT consultant or team has limited time for dissemination of information to other district personnel.	District does not support training of AT consultant or team or provide time for AT activities.
F. Staff members and parents monitor and adjust implementation according to changing student needs/abilities.	All students are followed closely by team (including parents) with AT support on a consistent basis.	Monitoring by team (including parents) on a consistent basis. AT consultant assists as needed.	Monitoring and adjusting done by team, but parents are not normally involved.	Teacher monitors and adjusts without team support. No formal input from parents.	AT monitoring only takes place at annual IEP review.

(continued next page)

COMPONENTS OF EFFECTIVE ASSISTIVE TECHNOLOGY SERVICE DELIVERY	HIGHLY SATISFACTORY		VARIATIONS		NEEDS IMPROVEMENT
	(5)	(4)	(3)	(2)	(1)
6. PERIODIC REVIEW					
A. Student AT use is reviewed and evaluated.	Each student's AT use is regularly evaluated, to determine changes needed.	Each student's AT use is reviewed on a generally consistent schedule.	Student progress with AT is reviewed in preparation for the annual IEP meeting.	Some students' AT use is reviewed but generally only when a parent expresses concern.	Effectiveness is not reviewed. Goals may be repeated in IEPs from year to year.
B. The district's AT services are reviewed on a regular schedule.	The AT services are reviewed on same schedule as other district programs.	The AT services are occasionally reviewed.	AT services have been reviewed in the past.	Some service providers or teams review aggregated data for AT use.	AT services have never been reviewed across district/agency.
C. AT is part of the district's overall technology plan.	AT is always included in technology planning across the district.	AT is usually included in technology plans.	AT is included only in some buildings or programs.	AT is only included in grants where its consideration is required.	AT is never included in planning for district technology needs.
D. Continuing education needs of staff are assessed and responded to by the district/ agency.	Need for new training in AT is regularly assessed and access to information arranged.	Need for training is occasionally assessed.	Need for training is responded to and supported when requested by staff.	Need for training is sometimes recognized.	Staff need for continued training in AT is not addressed.
7. TRANSITION					
A. Planning for transition includes specific consideration of AT needs.	Effective, systematic transition planning consistently includes AT when appropriate.	AT is frequently considered in transition planning.	AT is not generally included or considered in transition planning.	AT is rarely included or considered in transition planning.	AT is not part of, nor considered, in transition planning.
B. Advocacy, including self-advocacy, for AT use is addressed in transition planning.	AT advocacy and self-advocacy are part of instruction from an early age.	AT advocacy and self-advocacy are included in postsecondary transition.	AT advocacy is generally provided by school district staff, but self-advocacy is limited.	Advocacy and self-advocacy is taught, but its application is inconsistent.	Advocacy and self-advocacy is not taught or included in transition planning.

Source: Bowser, G., & Reed, P. (2017). Education Tech Points: Profile of AT Services in Schools. Winchester, OR: Coalition for Assistive Technology in Oregon. Retrieved from www.educationtechpoints.org/manuals-materials

Self-Evaluation Matrices for the Quality Indicators in Assistive Technology Services

Introduction to the QIAT Self-Evaluation Matrices

The Quality Indicators in Assistive Technology (QIAT) Self-Evaluation Matrices were developed in response to formative evaluation data indicating a need for a model that could assist in the application of the Quality Indicators for Assistive Technology Services in Schools (Zabala et al., 2000). The QIAT Matrices are based on the idea that change does not happen immediately, but rather, moves toward the ideal in a series of steps that take place over time. The QIAT Matrices use the Innovation Configuration Matrix (ICM) developed by Hall and Hord (1985) as a structural model. The ICM provides descriptive steps ranging from the unacceptable to the ideal that can be used as benchmarks to determine the current status of practice related to a specific goal or objective, and guide continuous improvement toward the ideal. It enables users to determine areas of strength that can be built upon as well as areas of challenge that need improvement.

When the QIAT Matrices are used to guide a collaborative self-assessment conducted by a diverse group of stakeholders within an agency, the information gained can be used to plan for changes that lead to improvement throughout the organization in manageable and attainable steps. The QIAT Matrices can also be used to evaluate the level to which expected or planned-for changes have taken place by periodically analyzing changes in service delivery over time.

When completed by an individual or team, the results of the self-assessment can be used to measure areas of strength and plan for needed professional development, training, or support for the individual or team. When an individual or team uses the QIAT Matrices, however, it is important to realize that the results can only reasonably reflect perceptions of the services in which that individual or team is involved and may not reflect the typical services within the organization. Since a primary goal of QIAT is to increase the quality and consistency of assistive technology (AT) services to *all* students throughout the organization, the perception that an individual or small group is working at the level of best practices does not necessarily mean that the need for quality and consistency of services has been met throughout the organization. The descriptive steps included in the QIAT Matrices are meant to provide illustrative examples and may not be specifically appropriate, as written, for all environments. People using the QIAT Matrices may wish to revise the descriptive steps to align them more closely for specific environments. However, when doing this, care must be taken that the revised steps do not compromise the intent of the quality indictor to which they apply.

The QIAT Matrices document is a companion document to the list of Quality Indicators and Intent Statements. The original six indicator areas were validated by research in 2004 and revisions were made in 2005, 2012, and 2015. For more information, please refer to the indicators and intent statements on the QIAT website at *www.qiat.org*. Before an item in the QIAT Matrices is discussed and rated, we recommend the groups read the entire item in the list of Quality Indicators and Intent Statements so that the intent of the item is clear.

References

Hall, G. E. and Hord, S. M. (1987) *Change in Schools: Facilitating the Process.* Ithaca: State University of New York Press.

QIAT Community. (2015). Quality indicators for assistive technology services. Retrieved April 5, 2015 from *http://qiat.org/indicators.html*

Zabala, J. S. (2007). *Development and evaluation of quality indicators for assistive technology services.* University of Kentucky Doctoral Dissertations. Paper 517. Retrieved from *http://uknowledge.uky.edu/gradschool_diss/517*

Zabala, J. S., Bowser, G., Blunt, M., Carl, D. F., Davis, S., Deterding, C., Foss, T., Korsten, J., Hamman, T., Hartsell, K., Marfilius, S. W., McCloskey-Dale, S., Nettleton, S. D., & Reed, P. (2000). Quality indicators for assistive technology services. *Journal of Special Education Technology, 15*(4), 25-36.

Zabala, J. S., & Carl, D. F. (2005). Quality indicators for assistive technology services in schools. In D.L. Edyburn, K. Higgins, & R. Boone (Eds.), *The handbook of special education technology research and practice* (pp. 179-207). Whitefish Bay, WI: Knowledge by Design, Inc.

Quality Indicators for *Consideration* of Assistive Technology Needs

QUALITY INDICATOR	UNACCEPTABLE		
1. Assistive technology (AT) devices and services are *considered for all students with disabilities* regardless of type or severity of disability.	1 AT is not considered for students with disabilities.	2 AT is considered only for students with severe disabilities or students in specific disability categories.	
2. During the development of the individualized educational program (IEP), every IEP team consistently uses a *collaborative decision-making process* that supports systematic consideration of each student's possible need for AT devices and services.	1 No process is established for IEP teams to use to make AT decisions.	2 A process is established for IEP teams to use to make AT decisions but it is not collaborative.	
3. IEP team members have the *collective knowledge and skills* needed to make informed AT decisions and seek assistance when needed.	1 The team does not have the knowledge or skills needed to make informed AT decisions. The team does not seek help when needed.	2 Individual team members have some of the knowledge and skills needed to make informed AT decisions. The team does not seek help when needed.	
4. Decisions regarding the need for AT devices and services *are based on the student's IEP goals and objectives, access to curricular and extracurricular activities, and progress in the general education curriculum.*	1 Decisions about a student's need for AT are not connected to IEP goals or the general curriculum.	2 Decisions about a student's need for AT are based on either access to the curriculum/IEP goals or the general curriculum, not both.	
5. The IEP team *gathers and analyzes data* about the student, customary environments, educational goals, and tasks when considering a student's need for AT devices and services.	1 The IEP team does not gather and analyze data to consider a student's need for AT devices and services.	2 The IEP team gathers and analyzes data about the student, customary environments, educational goals, or tasks, but not all, when considering a student's need for AT devices and services.	
6. When AT is needed, the IEP team *explores a range* of AT devices, services, and other supports that address identified needs.	1 The IEP team does not explore a range of AT devices, services, and other supports to address identified needs.	2 The IEP team considers a limited set of AT devices, services, and other supports.	
7. The AT consideration process and *results are documented in the IEP* and include a rationale for the decision and supporting evidence.	1 The consideration process and results are not documented in the IEP.	2 The consideration process and results are documented in the IEP but do not include a rationale for the decision and supporting evidence.	

3	4	5
AT is considered for all students with disabilities but the consideration is inconsistently based on the unique educational needs of the student.	AT is considered for all students with disabilities and the consideration is generally based on the unique educational needs of the student.	AT is considered for all students with disabilities and the consideration is consistently based on the unique educational needs of the student.
3	4	5
A collaborative process is established but not generally used by IEP teams to make AT decisions.	A collaborative process is established and generally used by IEP teams to make AT decisions.	A collaborative process is established and consistently used by IEP teams to make AT decisions.
3	4	5
Team members sometimes combine knowledge and skills to make informed AT decisions. The team does not always seek help when needed.	Team members generally combine their knowledge and skills to make informed AT decisions. The team seeks help when needed.	The team consistently uses collective knowledge and skills to make informed AT decisions. The team seeks help when needed.
3	4	5
Decisions about a student's need for AT sometimes are based on both the student's IEP goals and general education curricular tasks.	Decisions about a student's need for AT generally are based on both the student's IEP goals and general education curricular tasks.	Decisions about a student's need for AT consistently are based on both the student's IEP goals and general education curricular tasks.
3	4	5
The IEP team sometimes gathers and analyzes data about the student, customary environments, educational goals, and tasks when considering a student's need for AT devices and services.	The IEP team generally gathers and analyzes data about the student, customary environments, educational goals, and tasks when considering a student's need for AT devices and services.	The IEP team consistently gathers and analyzes data about the student, customary environments, educational goals, and tasks when considering a student's need for AT devices and services.
3	4	5
The IEP team sometimes explores a range of AT devices, services, and other supports.	The IEP team generally explores a range of AT devices, services, and other supports.	The IEP team always explores a range of AT devices, services, and other supports to address identified needs.
3	4	5
The consideration process and results are documented in the IEP and sometimes include a rationale for the decision and supporting evidence.	The consideration process and results are documented in the IEP and generally include a rationale for the decision and supporting evidence.	The consideration process and results are documented in the IEP and consistently include a rationale for the decision and supporting evidence.

Quality Indicators for *Assessment* of Assistive Technology Needs

QUALITY INDICATOR	UNACCEPTABLE		
1. *Procedures* for all aspects of AT assessment are clearly defined and consistently applied.	1 No procedures are defined.	2 Some assessment procedures are defined, but not generally used.	
2. AT assessments are conducted by a *team with the collective knowledge and skills needed* to determine possible AT solutions that address the needs and abilities of the student, demands of the customary environments, educational goals, and related activities.	1 A designated individual with no prior knowledge of the student's needs or technology conducts assessments.	2 A designated person or group conducts assessments but lacks either knowledge of AT or of the student's needs, environments, or tasks.	
3. All AT assessments include a functional assessment in the student's *customary environments*, such as the classroom, lunchroom, playground, home, community setting, or work place.	1 No component of the AT assessment is conducted in any of the student's customary environments.	2 No component of the AT assessment is conducted in any of the customary environments; however, data about the customary environments are sought.	
4. AT assessments, including needed trials, are completed within *reasonable timelines*.	1 AT assessments are not completed within agency timelines.	2 AT assessments are frequently out of compliance with timelines.	
5. Recommendations from AT assessments are *based on data* about the student, environments, and tasks.	1 Recommendations are not data-based.	2 Recommendations are based on incomplete data from limited sources.	
6. The assessment provides the IEP team with clearly *documented recommendations* that guide decisions about the selection, acquisition, and use of AT devices and services.	1 Recommendations are not documented.	2 Documented recommendations include only devices. Recommendations about services are not documented.	
7. AT needs are *reassessed* anytime changes in the student, the environments, and/or the tasks result in the student's needs not being met with current devices or services.	1 AT needs are not reassessed.	2 AT needs are only reassessed when requested. Reassessment is done formally and no ongoing AT assessment takes place.	

		PROMISING PRACTICES
3 Procedures are defined and used only by specialized personnel.	4 Procedures are clearly defined and generally used in both special and general education.	5 Everyone involved in the assessment process uses clearly defined procedures.
3 A team conducts assessments with limited input from individuals who have knowledge of AT or of the student's needs, environments, and tasks.	4 A collaborative team whose members have direct knowledge of the student's needs, environments, and tasks, and knowledge of AT generally conducts assessments.	5 A collaborative, flexible team formed on the basis of knowledge of the individual student's needs, environments, and tasks, and expertise in AT consistently conducts assessments.
3 Functional components of AT assessments are sometimes conducted in the student's customary environments.	4 Functional components of AT assessments are generally conducted in the student's customary environments.	5 Functional components of AT assessments are consistently conducted in the student's customary environments.
3 AT assessments are completed within a reasonable timeline and may or may not include initial trials.	4 AT assessments are completed within a reasonable timeline and include at least initial trials.	5 AT assessments are conducted in a timely manner and include a plan for ongoing assessment and trials in customary environments.
3 Recommendations are sometimes based on data about student performance on typical tasks in customary environments.	4 Recommendations are generally based on data about student performance on typical tasks in customary environments.	5 Recommendations are consistently based on data about student performance on typical tasks in customary environments.
3 Documented recommendations may or may not include sufficient information about devices and services to guide decision-making and program development.	4 Documented recommendations generally include sufficient information about devices and services to guide decision-making and program development.	5 Documented recommendations consistently include sufficient information about devices and services to guide decision-making and program development.
3 AT needs are reassessed on an annual basis or upon request. Reassessment may include some ongoing and formal assessment strategies.	4 AT use is frequently monitored. AT needs are generally reassessed if current tools and strategies are ineffective. Reassessment generally includes ongoing assessment strategies and includes formal assessment, if indicated.	5 AT use is frequently monitored. AT needs are generally reassessed if current tools and strategies are ineffective. Reassessment generally includes ongoing assessment strategies and includes formal assessment, if indicated.

Quality Indicators for Including Assistive Technology in the IEP

QUALITY INDICATOR	UNACCEPTABLE		
1. The education agency has *guidelines for documenting* **AT needs in the IEP and requires their consistent application.**	1 The agency does not have guidelines for documenting AT in the IEP.	2 The agency has guidelines for documenting AT in the IEP but team members are not aware of them.	
2. All *services* **that the IEP team determines are needed to support the selection, acquisition, and use of AT devices are designated in the IEP.**	1 AT devices and services are not documented in the IEP.	2 Some AT devices and services are minimally documented. Documentation does not include sufficient information to support effective implementation.	
3. The IEP illustrates that AT is a *tool to support achievement of goals* **and progress in the general curriculum by establishing a clear relationship between the student's needs, AT devices and services, and the student's goals and objectives.**	1 AT use is not linked to IEP goals and objectives or participation and progress in the general curriculum.	2 AT use is sometimes linked to IEP goals and objectives but not linked to the general curriculum.	
4. IEP content regarding AT use is written in language that describes how AT contributes to achievement of *measurable and observable outcomes.*	1 The IEP does not describe outcomes to be achieved through AT use.	2 The IEP describes outcomes to be achieved through AT use, but they are not measurable.	
5. AT is included in the IEP in a manner that provides a *clear and complete* **description of the devices and services to be provided and is used to address student needs and achieve expected results.**	1 Devices and services needed to support AT use are not documented.	2 Some devices and services are documented but they do not adequately support AT use.	

3	4	5
The agency has guidelines for documenting AT in the IEP and members of some teams are aware of them.	The agency has guidelines for documenting AT in the IEP and members of most teams are aware of them.	The agency has guidelines for documenting AT in the IEP and members of all teams are aware of them.
3	4	5
Required AT devices and services are documented. Documentation sometimes includes sufficient information to support effective implementation.	Required AT devices and services are documented. Documentation generally includes sufficient information to support effective implementation.	Required AT devices and services are documented. Documentation consistently includes sufficient information to support effective implementation.
3	4	5
AT use is linked to IEP goals and objectives and sometimes linked to the general curriculum.	AT use is linked to IEP goals and objectives and is generally linked to the general curriculum.	AT use is linked to the IEP goals and objectives and is consistently linked to the general curriculum.
3	4	5
The IEP describes outcomes to be achieved through AT use, but only some are measurable.	The IEP generally describes observable, measurable outcomes to be achieved through AT use.	The IEP consistently describes observable, measurable outcomes to be achieved through AT use.
3	4	5
Devices and services are documented and are sometime adequate to support AT use.	Devices and services are documented and are generally adequate to support AT use.	Devices and services are documented and are consistently adequate to support AT use.

Quality Indicators for Assistive Technology *Implementation*

QUALITY INDICATOR	UNACCEPTABLE		
1. AT implementation proceeds according to a *collaboratively developed plan*.	1 There is no implementation plan.	2 Individual team members may develop AT implementation plans independently.	
2. AT is *integrated* into the curriculum and daily activities of the student across environments.	1 AT included in the IEP is rarely used.	2 AT is used in isolation with no links to the student's curriculum and/or daily activities.	
3. Persons supporting the student across all environments in which the AT is expected to be used *share responsibility* for implementation of the plan.	1 Responsibility for implementation is not accepted by any team member.	2 Responsibility for implementation is assigned to one team member.	
4. Persons supporting the student provide opportunities for the student to use *a variety of strategies—including AT*—and to learn which strategies are most effective for particular circumstances and tasks.	1 No strategies are provided to support the accomplishment of tasks.	2 Only one strategy is provided to support the accomplishment of tasks.	
5. *Learning opportunities* for the student, family, and staff are an integral part of implementation.	1 AT needs for learning opportunities have not been determined.	2 AT learning opportunity needs are initially identified for student, family, and staff, but no training has been provided.	
6. AT implementation is initially based on assessment *data* and is adjusted based on performance data.	1 AT implementation is based on equipment availability and limited knowledge of team members, not on student data.	2 AT implementation is loosely based on initial assessment data and rarely adjusted.	
7. AT implementation includes management and maintenance of equipment and materials.	1 Equipment and materials are not managed or maintained. Students rarely have access to the equipment and materials they require.	2 Equipment and materials are managed and maintained on a crisis basis. Students frequently do not have access to the equipment and materials they require.	

3 Some team members collaborate in the development of an AT implementation plan.	4 Most team members collaborate in the development of AT implementation plan.	5 All team members collaborate in the development of a comprehensive AT implementation plan.
3 AT is sometimes integrated into the student's curriculum and daily activities.	4 AT is generally integrated into the student's curriculum and daily activities.	5 AT is fully integrated into the student's curriculum and daily activities.
3 Responsibility for implementation is shared by some team members in some environments.	4 Responsibility for implementation is generally shared by most team members in most environments.	5 Responsibility for implementation is consistently shared among team members across all environments.
3 Multiple strategies are provided. Students are sometimes encouraged to select and use the most appropriate strategy for each task.	4 Multiple strategies are provided. Students are generally encouraged to select and use the most appropriate strategy for each task.	5 Multiple strategies are provided. Students are consistently encouraged to select and use the most appropriate strategy for each task.
3 Initial AT learning opportunities are sometimes provided to student, family, and staff.	4 Initial and follow-up AT learning opportunities are generally provided to student, family, and staff	5 Ongoing AT learning opportunities are provided to student, family, and staff as needed, based on changing needs.
3 AT implementation is based on initial assessment data and is sometimes adjusted as needed based on student progress.	4 AT implementation is based on initial assessment data and is generally adjusted as needed based on student progress.	5 AT implementation is based on initial assessment data and is consistently adjusted as needed based on student progress.
3 Equipment and materials are managed and maintained so that students sometimes have access to the equipment and materials they require.	4 Equipment and materials are managed and maintained so that students generally have access to the equipment and materials they require.	5 Equipment and materials are effectively managed and maintained so that students consistently have access to the equipment and materials they require.

Quality Indicators for *Evaluation of the Effectiveness* of Assistive Technology

QUALITY INDICATOR	UNACCEPTABLE	
1. Team members share *clearly defined responsibilities* to ensure that data are collected, evaluated, and interpreted by capable and credible team members.	1 Responsibilities for data collection, evaluation, or interpretation are not defined.	2 Responsibilities for data collection, evaluation, or interpretation of data are assigned to one team member.
2. Data are collected on specific student achievement that has been identified by the team and is *related to one or more goals*.	1 Team neither identifies specific changes in student behaviors expected from AT use nor collects data.	2 Team identifies student behaviors and collects data, but the behaviors are either not specific or not related to IEP goals.
3. Evaluation of effectiveness includes the *quantitative and qualitative* measurement of changes in the student's performance and achievement.	1 Effectiveness is not evaluated.	2 Evaluation of effectiveness is based not on student performance, but rather on subjective opinion.
4. Effectiveness is evaluated *across environments* including during naturally occurring opportunities as well as structured activities.	1 Effectiveness is not evaluated in any environment.	2 Effectiveness is evaluated only during structured opportunities in controlled environments (e.g., massed trials data).
5. Data are collected so teams can analyze *student achievement and identify supports and barriers* that influence AT use and determine what changes, if any, are needed.	1 No data are collected or analyzed.	2 Data are collected but are not analyzed.
6. *Changes are made* in the student's AT services and educational program when evaluation data indicate that such changes are needed to improve student achievement.	1 Program changes are never made.	2 Program changes are made in the absence of data.
7. Evaluation of effectiveness is a dynamic, responsive, *ongoing process* that is reviewed periodically.	1 No process is used to evaluate effectiveness.	2 Evaluation of effectiveness only takes place annually, but the team does not make program changes based on data.

		PROMISING PRACTICES
3 Responsibilities for collection, evaluation, and interpretation of data are shared by some team members.	4 Responsibilities for collection, evaluation, and interpretation of data are shared by most team members.	5 Responsibilities for collection, evaluation, and interpretation of data are consistently shared by team members.
3 Team identifies specific student behaviors related to IEP goals, but inconsistently collects data.	4 Team identifies specific student behaviors related to IEP goals, and generally collects data.	5 Team identifies specific student behaviors related to IEP goals, and consistently collects data on changes in those behaviors.
3 Evaluation of effectiveness is not consistent or is based on limited data about student performance.	4 Evaluation of effectiveness is generally based on quantitative and qualitative data about student performance from a few sources.	5 Effectiveness is consistently evaluated using both quantitative and qualitative data about student's performance obtained from a variety of sources.
3 Effectiveness is evaluated during structured activities across environments and a few naturally occurring opportunities.	4 Effectiveness is generally evaluated during naturally occurring opportunities and structured activities in multiple environments.	5 Effectiveness is consistently evaluated during naturally occurring opportunities and structured activities in multiple environments.
3 Data are superficially analyzed.	4 Data are sufficiently analyzed most of the time.	5 Data are sufficiently analyzed all of the time.
3 Program changes are loosely linked to student performance data.	4 Program changes are generally linked to student performance data.	5 Program changes are consistently linked to student performance data.
3 Evaluation of effectiveness only takes place annually and the team uses the data to make annual program changes	4 Evaluation of effectiveness takes place on an on-going basis and team generally uses the data to make program changes.	5 Evaluation of effectiveness takes place on an on-going basis and the team consistently uses the data to make program changes.

Quality Indicators for Assistive Technology in *Transition*

QUALITY INDICATOR	UNACCEPTABLE		
1. *Transition plans address the AT needs* of the student, including roles and training needs of team members, subsequent steps in AT use, and follow-up after transition takes place.	1 Transition plans do not address AT needs.	2 Transition plans rarely address AT needs, critical roles, steps, or follow-up.	
2. Transition *planning empowers the student* using AT to participate in the transition planning at a level appropriate to age and ability.	1 Student is not present.	2 Student may be present but does not participate or input is ignored.	
3. *Advocacy related to AT use is recognized as critical* and planned for by the teams involved in transition.	1 No one advocates for AT use or the development of student self-determination skills.	2 Advocacy rarely occurs for AT use or the development of student self-determination skills.	
4. *AT requirements in the receiving environment* are identified during the transition planning process.	1 AT requirements in the receiving environment are not identified.	2 AT requirements in the receiving environment are rarely identified.	
5. Transition planning for students using AT proceeds according to an *individualized timeline.*	1 Individualized timelines are not developed to support transition planning for students using AT.	2 Individualized timelines are developed, but do not support transition planning for students using AT.	
6. Transition plans address specific *equipment, training, and funding* issues, such as transfer or acquisition of AT, manuals, and support documents.	1 The plans do not address AT equipment, training, and funding issues.	2 The plans rarely address AT equipment, training, and/or funding issues.	

		PROMISING PRACTICES
3 Transition plans sometimes address AT needs but may not include critical roles, steps, or follow-up.	4 Transition plans always address AT needs and usually include critical roles, steps, or follow-up.	5 Transition plans consistently address AT needs and all team members are involved and knowledgeable about critical roles, steps, and follow-up.
3 Student sometimes participates and some student input is considered.	4 Student participates and student input is generally reflected in the transition plan.	5 Student is a full participant and student input is consistently reflected in the transition plan.
3 Advocacy sometimes occurs for AT use and the development of student self-determination skills.	4 Advocacy usually occurs for AT use and the development of student self-determination skills.	5 Advocacy consistently occurs for AT use and the development of student self-determination skills.
3 AT requirements in the receiving environment are identified, some participants are involved, and some requirements are addressed.	4 AT requirements in the receiving environment are identified, most participants are involved, and most requirements are addressed.	5 AT requirements in the receiving environment are consistently identified by all participants.
3 Individualized timelines are sometimes developed and support transition planning for students using AT.	4 Individualized timelines are generally developed and support transition planning for students using AT.	5 Individualized timelines are consistently developed and support transition planning for students using AT.
3 The plans sometimes address AT equipment, training, or funding issues.	4 The plans usually address AT equipment, training, and funding issues.	5 The plans consistently address AT equipment, training, and funding issues.

Quality Indicators for *Administrative Support* of Assistive Technology

QUALITY INDICATOR	UNACCEPTABLE		
1. The education agency has *written procedural guidelines* that ensure equitable access to AT devices and services for students with disabilities, if required for a free appropriate public education (FAPE).	1 No written procedural guidelines are in place.	2 Written procedural guidelines for few components of AT service delivery (e.g., assessment or consideration) are in place.	
2. The education agency *broadly disseminates* clearly defined procedures for accessing and providing AT services, and supports the implementation of those guidelines.	1 No procedures disseminated and no plan to disseminate.	2 A plan for dissemination exists, but has not been implemented.	
3. The education agency includes appropriate AT responsibilities in *written descriptions of job requirements* for each position in which activities impact AT services.	1 No job requirements relating to AT are written.	2 Job requirements related to AT are written only for a few specific personnel who provide AT services.	
4. The education agency employs *personnel with the competencies* needed to support quality AT services within their primary areas of responsibility at all levels of the organization.	1 AT competencies are not considered in hiring, assigning, or evaluating personnel.	2 AT competencies are recognized as an added value in an employee but are not sought.	
5. The education agency includes *AT in the technology planning and budgeting process.*	1 There is no planning and budgeting process for AT.	2 AT planning and budgeting is a special education function that is not included in the agency-wide technology planning and budgeting process.	
6. The education agency provides access to *ongoing learning opportunities about AT* for staff, family, and students.	1 No learning opportunities related to AT are provided.	2 Learning opportunities related to AT are provided on a crisis-basis only. Learning opportunities may not be available to all who need them.	
7. The education agency uses a *systematic process to evaluate* all components of the agency-wide AT program.	1 The agency-wide AT program is not evaluated.	2 Varying procedures are used to evaluate some components of the agency-wide AT program.	

3 Written procedural guidelines that address several components of AT service delivery are in place.	4 Written procedural guidelines that address most components of AT service delivery are in place.	5 Comprehensive written procedural guidelines that address all components of AT service delivery are in place.
3 Procedures are disseminated to a few staff who work directly with AT.	4 Procedures are disseminated to most agency personnel and generally used.	5 Procedures are disseminated to all agency personnel and consistently used.
3 Job requirements related to AT are written for most personnel who provide AT services but are not clearly aligned to job responsibilities.	4 Job requirements related to AT are written for most personnel who provide AT services and are generally aligned to job responsibilities.	5 Job requirements related to AT are written for all personnel who provide AT services and are clearly aligned to job responsibilities.
3 AT competencies are recognized and sought for specific personnel.	4 AT competencies are generally valued and used in hiring, assigning, and evaluating personnel.	5 AT competencies are consistently valued and used in hiring, assigning, and evaluating personnel.
3 AT is sometimes included in the agency-wide technology planning and budgeting process, but in a way that is inadequate to meet AT needs throughout the agency.	4 AT is generally included in agency-wide technology planning and budgeting process in a way that meets most AT needs throughout the agency.	5 AT is included in the agency-wide technology planning and budgeting process in a way that meets AT needs throughout the agency.
3 Learning opportunities related to AT are provided to some individuals on a pre-defined schedule.	4 Learning opportunities related to AT are provided on a pre-defined schedule to most individuals with some follow-up opportunities.	5 Learning opportunities related to AT are provided on an ongoing basis to address the changing needs of students with disabilities, their families, and the staff who serve them.
3 A systematic procedure is inconsistently used to evaluate a few components of the agency-wide AT program.	4 A systematic procedure is generally used to evaluate most components of the agency-wide AT program.	5 A systematic procedure is consistently used throughout the agency to evaluate all components of the agency-wide AT program.

Quality Indicators for *Professional Development and Training* in Assistive Technology

QUALITY INDICATOR	UNACCEPTABLE	
1. Comprehensive AT professional development and training *support the understanding that AT devices and services enable students to accomplish IEP goals and objectives and make progress in the general curriculum.*	1 There is no professional development and training in the use of AT.	2 Professional development and training address only technical aspects of AT tools and/or are not related to use for academic achievement.
2. The education agency has an AT professional development and training plan that *identifies the audiences, purposes, activities, expected results, evaluation measures, and funding* for AT professional development and training.	1 There is no plan for AT professional development and training.	2 The plan includes unrelated activities done on a sporadic basis for a limited audience.
3. AT professional development and training address and are *aligned with other local, state, and national professional development initiatives.*	1 Professional development and training do not consider other initiatives.	2 Professional development and training rarely align with other initiatives.
4. AT professional development and *training include ongoing learning opportunities that utilize local, regional, and/ or national resources.*	1 There are no professional development and training opportunities.	2 Professional development and training occur infrequently.
5. Professional development and training in AT follow *research-based models for adult learning* **that include multiple formats and are delivered at multiple skill levels.**	1 Professional development and training never consider adult learning.	2 Professional development and training rarely consider models for adult learning strategies.
6. The effectiveness of AT professional development and training is *evaluated by measuring changes* **in practice that result in improved student performance.**	1 Changes in practice are not measured.	2 Changes in practice are rarely measured.

3 Some professional development and training include strategies for use of AT devices and services to facilitate academic achievement.	4 Most professional development and training include strategies for use of AT devices and services to facilitate academic achievement.	5 All professional development and training include strategies for use of AT devices and services to facilitate academic achievement.
3 The plan includes some elements (e.g., variety of activities, purpose, levels) for some audiences.	4 The plan includes most elements of a comprehensive plan for most audiences.	5 The comprehensive AT professional development plan encompasses all elements, audiences, and levels.
3 Professional development and training sometimes align with other initiatives.	4 Professional development and training generally align with other initiatives.	5 Professional development and training consistently align with other initiatives as appropriate.
3 Professional development and training are sometimes provided.	4 Professional development and training are generally provided.	5 Professional development and training opportunities are provided on a comprehensive, repetitive, and continuous schedule, utilizing appropriate local, regional, and national resources.
3 Professional development and training sometimes consider research-based adult learning strategies.	4 Professional development and training generally consider research-based adult learning strategies.	5 Professional development and training consistently consider research-based adult learning strategies.
3 Changes in practice are measured using a variety of measures but may not be related to student performance.	4 Changes in practice are usually measured using a variety of reliable measures linked to improved student performance.	5 Changes in practice are consistently measured using a variety of reliable measures linked to improved student performance.

AT Leadership Self-Rating

LEADERSHIP FOR AT SERVICES	SELF-RATING			
Know what AT is and how it can benefit students with disabilities.	1	2	3	4
Know who the AT leaders are in the agency and work with them directly to develop, maintain, and improve AT services.	1	2	3	4
Know the legal definitions of AT, the requirements to provide AT for students with disabilities, and the implications for my program.	1	2	3	4
Help staff, students, and families develop a vision for AT use and communicate that vision widely.	1	2	3	4
Support faculty and staff in using AT to improve the education of students with disabilities.	1	2	3	4
Develop a culture where AT devices and services are valued and used.	1	2	3	4
Facilitate and support collaboration between departments to improve learning for student with disabilities through the use of AT.	1	2	3	4
Ensure equity of access to AT devices and services for students of all ages, disabilities, and school placements.	1	2	3	4
MANAGEMENT FOR AT SERVICES	**SELF-RATING**			
Develop, implement, and monitor policies and written operating guidelines for providing AT services.	1	2	3	4
Ensure that written guidelines include processes for AT consideration during the IEP meeting, AT assessment, and implementation of AT plans.	1	2	3	4
Ensure that all appropriate employees know how to respond to a parent's request for AT.	1	2	3	4
Require that staff use data to make AT decisions.	1	2	3	4
Make available planning time, funds, and human resources for the provision of AT services.	1	2	3	4
Upgrade the AT inventory as needed.	1	2	3	4
Monitor AT services to ensure they are provided in a cost-effective and efficient manner.	1	2	3	4

SUPERVISION FOR AT SERVICES	SELF-RATING			
Assess staff AT knowledge, skills, performance, and training needs.	1	2	3	4
Recruit individuals with AT skills.	1	2	3	4
Ensure that all staff, including general education teachers, have the necessary understanding of AT to fulfill their role in supporting the use of AT by students with disabilities in their classes.	1	2	3	4
Demonstrate interest and support for making AT available and usable by students as part of staff evaluation and supervision.	1	2	3	4
Ensure that all staff members who serve a child with a disability implement the IEP, including any use of AT, in a legal and ethical manner.	1	2	3	4
Foster a school environment that has a low level of conflict and assist in conflict resolution, including conflict about AT.	1	2	3	4
Support teams as they work to make AT available to students with disabilities by providing structure and clear expectations.	1	2	3	4
ADVOCACY AND PROGRAM IMPROVEMENT FOR AT SERVICES	SELF-RATING			
Advocate for AT services and resources at school board meetings, administrative staff meetings, community forums, parent organizations, and professional organizations.	1	2	3	4
Develop, implement, and monitor a long-range and system-wide AT plan.	1	2	3	4
Use research-based program improvement strategies, including the Plan-Do-Study-Act cycle.	1	2	3	4
Conduct ongoing evaluation of AT services in the same way as other services are evaluated.	1	2	3	4
Integrate AT into strategic plans, technology plans, and other improvement plans and policies to align efforts and leverage resources.	1	2	3	4

Index

CPSIA information can be obtained
at www.ICGtesting.com
Printed in the USA
LVHW011747200422
716609LV00012B/976

9 781930 583108